Portrait of Ngaio Marsh, 1981 by Vy Elsom.
Oil on canvas. Size: Actual 810 x 610 mm; Framed 945 x 745 mm.
Collection of the Robert McDougall Art Gallery, Christchurch, NZ.
Presented by the artist, February 1983. Photograph by Merilyn Hooper.

NGAIO MARSH
The Woman and Her Work

edited by
B. J. RAHN

The Scarecrow Press, Inc.
Metuchen, N.J., & London
1995

British Library Cataloguing-in-Publication Data available

Library of Congress Cataloging-in-Publication Data

Ngaio Marsh : the woman and her work / edited by B. J. Rahn.
    p.   cm.
Includes bibliographical references (p.).
ISBN 0-8108-3023-X
    1. Marsh, Ngaio. 1895-1982.   2. Detective and mystery stories. New
Zealand--History and criticism.   3. Women theatrical producers and
directors--New Zealand--Biography.   4. Women and literature--New
Zealand--History--20th century.   5. Women authors. New Zealand--
20th century--Biography.   I. Rahn, B. J. (Beverly Jean), 1934-
PR9639.3.M27Z83 1995
823--dc20
    [B]   95-5785

Dedication

In loving memory of my father, Carl H. Rahn, who introduced me to the pleasures of storytelling as a child and, consequently, enriched my life beyond measure.

Table of Contents

Detective Fiction: A Mirror of Social History

Short Fiction

Appendixes

Acknowledgments

I should like, first of all, to thank the contributors to this festschrift, who have given so generously of their time, advice, and knowledge. Without them, it would not exist.

Special kudos go to Mr. Colin McLachlan of the Ngaio Marsh House and Heritage Trust, who put me in touch with the two New Zealanders who have written articles for this collection. I especially appreciate the trust and good will of these kindly folk from the antipodes who undertook this project without ever having met the editor.

In addition, I owe a debt of gratitude to Brian Stone of Aitken, Stone & Wylie, the literary agent for the Ngaio Marsh Estate, who smoothed the way for me by granting permission to quote from the texts of Ngaio Marsh's novels and by allowing me to choose photographs from his firm's files for publication herein. A special thank you goes to his assistant, Katie McKay, who cut a path through the thicket of red tape regarding their use.

Margaret Lewis, Paul Bushnell, and Bruce Harding have also located and generously arranged use of photographs from the Historic Places Trust, the Alexander Turnbull Library, the Macmillan Brown Library, and the Robert McDougall Art Gallery in New Zealand.

Finally, I should like to thank a former student, Catherine Kleinpeter, who typed some of the essays into the computer; Albert Del Bagnio and Jensene Payne, the good fairies of the fax machine in the office of the Dean of Humanities at Hunter College; and Professor Harvey Minkoff, my most critical advisor.

B. J. Rahn

Introduction

This book was created to celebrate the centenary of the birth of Edith Ngaio Marsh on 23 April 1995. Being born on St. George's Day, the putative birthday of William Shakespeare, seems to have influenced the future of Ngaio Marsh, for she grew to be a renowned director of Shakespeare's plays who inspired and guided two generations of actors and engendered love of Shakespeare's plays in New Zealand audiences for thirty years. Her talents received recognition first in 1948 when she was awarded an OBE (Officer of the Order of the British Empire) for services to literature and theatre, and later in 1967 when she was created DBE (Dame Commander of the Order of the British Empire). In 1962 she received the first honorary doctorate in literature conferred by the University of Canterbury in her native Christchurch, and in 1967 a new playhouse, the Ngaio Marsh Theatre, was named for her at the University.

Ngaio Marsh was born in the middle of the same decade as Agatha Christie and Dorothy L. Sayers, who were five and two years her senior respectively, and with them, she came to be regarded among the best writers of detective fiction of the Golden Age in England. To the delight of old and new readers, Marsh's thirty-two crime novels are continuously in print. For her literary achievements, she was presented with the Red Herrings Award in 1955 by the Crime Writers Association of the United Kingdom. In addition, she was voted a Grand Master and given an Edgar Award by the

Mystery Writers of America in 1978--the only female colonial writer to achieve such distinction.

A passionate supporter of the British Commonwealth, Ngaio Marsh became a public advocate of maintaining cultural bonds among member nations, especially through the arts. As a public figure she commanded international respect throughout the English-speaking world. Although essentially a shy person, Marsh was a woman of great charm; her personal charisma attracted many distinguished people, who subsequently became friends, into her orbit. Apart from her public and professional endeavors, in her personal life she was a devoted daughter, a loyal friend, and an inventive, fun-loving companion.

It seems fitting, on the occasion of her one hundredth birthday, that this multifaceted personality should be celebrated in a festschrift designed to honor Ngaio Marsh--the Woman and Her Work. Hence, this volume is divided into sections containing essays on Marsh's life, her career in the theatre, her detective novels, and her mystery short stories.

The biographical essays are written by her official biographer, Margaret Lewis; by a close family member, John Dacres-Mannings; and by two fellow detective authors who remember her fondly, H. R. F. Keating and Julian Symons. Lewis describes the challenge faced by the professional biographer who must form an understanding of an individual she has never met from official records, letters, diaries, and personal impressions provided by people acquainted with the subject. Dacres-Mannings provides the personal recollections of a kinsman who knew Marsh intimately over a long period of time. These two accounts offer contrasting biographical approaches--objective and subjective--thus representing Marsh from the outside and from the inside. Both Keating and Symons share memories of a literary tour with Marsh several years ago in the North of England, during which they both came to admire and like her and from which Symons emerged with a title for his current novel supplied by Marsh.

An overview of Marsh's involvement with the theatre from childhood onward is sketched by Paul Bushnell--with special emphasis on her Shakespearean triumphs. He comments on her lifelong love of Shakespeare, the early influence of Allan Wilkie on her directorial philosophy and style, her unique personal insights into the plays, her ability to inspire intense commitment and loyalty among the actors, and her insistence that Shakespeare's words, if spoken properly, inevitably communicate the intended meaning. He has also kindly supplied a chronological list of all of Marsh's productions (Appendix I). Marsh's interest in theatre spilled over into her detective novels with the result that she furnished some of her best known works with theatrical settings. Others focus on characters from show business and, as Marilyn Rye points out, in several more, dramatic presentations function as structural devices reflecting the tensions and relationships in the larger fictional world. Rye also draws parallels between the crime and a performance, with the perpetrator as an actor/director creating an illusion which Alleyn as audience/sleuth must penetrate to the reality beneath. Catherine Aird discusses a novel whose plot involves the rescue and rehabilitation of a decaying Victorian theatre which reopens with an original play based on the tragic death of Shakespeare's young son, Hamnet. Not only does Marsh indulge her love of the Bard, but she also utilizes her knowledge of theatre architecture and stagecraft and even prefaces the text with a list of dramatis personae. Aird revels in the richness of language in the dialogue of Marsh's characters on and off stage, pointing out its immediate evocation not only of theatre people and their milieu but also of the broader social context of the period.

Close scrutiny of Marsh's settings and her detective hero reveals the novels to be rich in social history, as do close readings of the texts. Alzina Stone Dale has discovered that Marsh's London settings are topographically realistic. The canvas stretches from Gravesend to the West End and beyond as far as Knightsbridge. Detailed painterly descriptions of locale evoke not only ambience but history, as when Marsh superimposes Shakespearean London at Blackfriars on the postwar London of Queen Elizabeth II. Marsh refers to well known London landmarks like Big Ben and Piccadilly Circus to invoke a general sense of environment, but Dale classifies particular London settings into two types: theatrical and autobiographical. Like Sayers, Marsh places her characters in neighborhoods where she had lived. Kathryne S. McDorman traces the origins of Marsh's unorthodox gentleman copper to actual developments within the police force at the time of Marsh's first visits to England. Socially, Roderick Alleyn signifies the transformation in attitudes toward class and professionalism in modern Britain; in the genre, Alleyn was a transitional figure foreshadowing the shift from the prewar well-born gifted amateur sleuth to the rank and file postwar professional policeman. McDorman notes characters' awareness of the incongruity between Alleyn's social class and his profession. She also interprets the bond between Alleyn and Fox as a triumph of professionalism over social class.

Both B. A. Pike and Susan Oleksiw examine characters' conversation and social behavior in a close textual analysis of the more serious social implications of two important novels of the early 1940's. In *Death of a Peer* (1940), as B. A. Pike observes, the inequities of the social class system are exposed in all their unlovely excesses and inadequacies. At the heart of the novel, the descendants of the old feudal order are weighed and found wanting; that is, they are unable to cope with the demands of the modern world outside their cosseted existence ensured by wealth and privilege. Their sense of justice is contaminated by their self interest. Their morals are dictated by personal feelings which admit no sense of abstract justice. In *Death and the Dancing Footman* (1941), the spectre of war in the background accentuates the silly pretensions, selfish desires, and petty conflicts of privileged guests in a classic country house murder mystery. According to Oleksiw, this novel discloses how quickly rational, civilized people revert to herd instinct when their security is threatened. Under pressure, they close ranks and allow distrust of the outsider to supplant rational social responsibility. It also deals with the masks people assume to hide personal flaws or acquire personal status or both. Oleksiw views the characters as the remnants of a moribund social order who follow a superficial code of etiquette, having abandoned the code of ethics upon which it is based.

Marsh's short stories are approached from different vantage points by Douglas G. Greene and Bruce Harding. Greene, editor of Marsh's collected short stories, reviews their publication history, assesses their literary merits, and discusses reasons for Marsh's difficulties with the short story form. Harding, on the other hand, investigates the circumstances which produced what he calls Marsh's amphibian nature and evaluates her unusual position as a colonial writer of "pure" English detective fiction. He traces dual cultural influences on Marsh's short fiction and identifies the ambivalent tensions she experienced which are apparent in her life and work.

Among the various pleasures of editing this festschrift, one of the chief has been the discovery of a certain fortuitous recursiveness among the contributors which provides both continuity and pleasure for the reader and imposes an inherent pattern of organization on the material for the editor. Without realizing who else was involved, each contributor wrote his/her essay on a topic of choice. The result was a group of articles in which authors made internal references to each other and in which a shared interest in certain themes and ideas is evident.

For example, Julian Symons recalls Marsh's reluctant acceptance of his request for a short story for a Detection Club anthology, *Verdict of Thirteen* (1978). Both Greene and Harding discuss this story, "Morepork." Symons's account offers confirmation of Greene's statement that Marsh found the short story form uncongenial, and confirms the basis for Harding's complaints that Symons's conditions for the story imposed artificial constraints and brought out Marsh's pro-English prejudices. Greene also endorses a theory posited by Margaret Lewis--based on Marsh's working habits--which explains her problems with the form.

In another instance, Kathryne McDorman defends detective fiction as a legitimate research source for social historians because detective novels are novels of manners. Catherine Aird's analysis of language in *Death at the Dolphin* supports McDorman's contention by revealing Marsh's novel, and others like it, to be repositories of social history, while Alzina Stone Dale's study of background validates the same argument with evidence drawn from setting. Pike and Oleksiw through scrutiny of the actual manners themselves demonstrate beyond dispute the claim that Marsh is a novelist of manners in a direct line of descent from Jane Austen through Charles Dickens and Dorothy L. Sayers. Harding quotes McDorman's remarks on Marsh's fileting of the English social class system but also points out that her observant eye extended to the social peccadillos of New Zealanders as well.

Marsh's divided efforts between the theatre and detective fiction as well as her divided existence between New Zealand and England, resulting in her divided allegiance, are identified by Lewis as essential to an understanding of her character, and they are discussed at length by Harding in terms of colonial ambivalence. But Rye takes this theme even further by suggesting that Marsh merged her creative interests in directing and writing in her theatrical detective novels. Rye also claims Marsh created a detective who mirrored her own sense of living a dual existence because he is always on the outside, merely an observer. And, like McDorman, Rye remarks on the reactions of other characters to Alleyn's anomalous position.

Recursion does not always indicate agreement, however. Greene and Harding differ regarding the significance of Marsh's short stories. Concurring with Lewis's judgment, Greene dismisses "Moonshine" as a sentimental tale more interesting as an autobiographical footnote on Marsh's lifelong love of Christmas than as a story; whereas, for Harding, lexical playfulness and formal excellence are outweighed by the autobiographical content which renders "Moonshine" more important than "Morepork." Dale takes exception to Lewis's assertion that the London of Marsh's detective novels is entirely fictitious, condemning it as inaccurate and anachronistic and maintaining that popular fiction often gives a surprisingly realistic portrait of the times.

Whether they agree or disagree with the interpretations and theories of the writers herein, I hope friends and admirers of Ngaio Marsh find this festschrift a fitting tribute to her and derive as much pleasure from reading it as I have from editing it.

B. J. Rahn, Ph.D.
Hunter College
New York City

Biography - Reminiscence

To Ngaio, from her biographer,
with affection and respect...

by Margaret Lewis

Caches in cupboards, boxes under beds, tidy bundles in desks and drawers--these papers and letters are the stuff of biography. Where would one be without the innate desire to hoard? Or, more seriously, without the need to preserve tangible relics of a friend whose memory inevitably fades as the years pass by? Biography brings to life these notes and letters, photographs and souvenirs, creating something new from disparate parts, something that has never existed before.

I embarked on the authorized biography of Dame Ngaio Marsh in 1987 five years after her death on 18 February 1982, having been invited to do so by the estate which looks after her literary interests. Gradually I built up a picture of her life, divided between two hemispheres, in New Zealand and in Europe, and two spheres of activity, writing detective fiction and directing plays, mainly Shakespeare, for the stage. The discovery of her early work as a painter was unexpectedly fascinating. Two lengthy research trips to New Zealand, and visits to the United States, France, and Australia helped me to fill in the details. *Ngaio Marsh: A Life* was published by Chatto and Windus in 1991, and at a launch party in London many of Ngaio's old friends joined to celebrate her memory. Among the group was Carmen Callil, then the formidable managing director of Chatto, and a great admirer of Ngaio Marsh, who had commissioned the book, encouraged me to

1

keep going and applied her keen eye to early drafts. Jimmy Laurenson, the actor, was there; the Reverend Simon Acland who delivered her funeral address; her relative "Bear" Mannings with his wife; Brian Stone, her present literary agent; and others who had known and worked with her. I was in the minority, as I had never known her. Yet I can truly say that the more I discovered about this remarkable woman with whom I became so intimate, whose tear-stained letters I read with sympathy, the more I came to admire her, and to appreciate the responsibility that I had been given in presenting her life to total strangers.

Despite my best efforts, many mysteries in the life of Ngaio Marsh remained unsolved. I suspect that most biographers, if honest, would admit that this is the case, yet many adopt the fashionably arrogant attitude that somehow they can know the mind of another person. I never believed that this was possible, and I am highly suspicious of those who make these claims.

I never knew, for instance, why Ngaio falsified her date of birth, steadfastly maintaining that it was 23 April, 1899, instead of the same date in 1895, through scores of reference books (including *Who's Who*) and interviews. Even when forced to reveal the truth in order to obtain her final navy-blue British passport in the 1970's, she later delicately scratched the real date of birth away and wrote in the fictitious year, 1899. Naturally I had checked all the family dates as one of the first tasks I undertook, so her real age was apparent from the beginning of my study. The altered passport did not emerge until I had been working for two years and it gave me quite a shock; such a proper lady should not have been defacing an official document. But this is the challenge of biography. As one gradually builds up the layers of a person's life, talking to relatives, to friends and to some enemies too, assembling the evidence, a picture begins to emerge like a photographic image gaining shape in a developer. The danger for a biographer is in bringing a pre-conceived shape to the task, and attempting to impose an outsider's judgement instead of allowing the person to emerge, in her own time, from the material. Clearly, to pretend to avoid any subjective judgement is ridiculous and would make for a very boring book. All biographers make judgements, both moral and aesthetic, as soon as they put pen to paper. But I feel that the biographer also has a duty to the subject to play fair and to play humanely. The reader can come to his or her own conclusions if the material is honestly delivered.

Although all but four of Ngaio Marsh's thirty-two novels are set in England, France, or Italy, I felt strongly that the key to understanding her work as a novelist and as a stage director lay in her New Zealand background. As someone who grew up within sight of the Canadian Rockies, I could appreciate why Ngaio always returned to her family home in Christchurch with its view across the city to the Southern Alps. Much as she loved those cozy southern English villages with their pretty cottages, quaint pubs and handsome manors set in beautiful gardens, the New Zealand landscape always called her back. The grandeur of the South Island and the clarity of the air are still extraordinary attributes.

Ngaio's childhood in New Zealand accounts for many of her attitudes in later life. Her mother, Rose Seager, was born in Christchurch in 1864, although her father, Henry Marsh was born in England and emigrated to New Zealand in 1888. Neither parent came from a wealthy background, despite Ngaio's fondness for allusions to aristocratic ancestry in England. Henry Marsh was the eldest son of a London tea broker whose business gradually declined, and Rose Seager was the daughter of Edward Seager, a remarkable man who served as a policeman in the New Zealand police force and later became supervisor of the new mental asylum outside

Christchurch. This gave rise to Ngaio's joke that some of her family were born in a lunatic asylum and some in jail, very true in the circumstances. From her maternal grandfather Ngaio inherited a great love of the stage and all kinds of entertainment. He ran a private theatre as part of his therapy for patients at the asylum, and as well as plays he put on conjuring shows, magic lantern performances and concerts. From her grandmother Ngaio inherited the ability to organize and deal with people. From her parents Ngaio learned a very particular, slightly restrictive, code of conduct. She also learned to value correct speech and she battled throughout her life with "New Zillan" accents, particularly as they affected her productions of Shakespeare. As with many people from her background, she was taught to think of England as "home" although she did not set eyes on the white cliffs of Dover until 1928, when she was thirty-three years old.

Ngaio was an only child and much cherished. Her father was a dreamy, gentle man who never rose above the position of clerk in the Bank of New Zealand in Christchurch where he worked all his life. Despite the need for many financial sacrifices, Ngaio was sent first to a private primary school, where her height and deep voice made her very self-conscious, and then to St. Margaret's College, a fee-paying Church of England school that had just opened in the city. Here she flourished, encountering for the first time girls of her own age who also liked painting, poetry and drama. One of the younger girls, Sylvia Fox, remained a close friend all her life.

At St. Margaret's, Ngaio was soon writing poetry and winning prizes for her essays. Her plays were performed to an audience of parents, and her mother, who was a talented amateur actor, took very seriously her role in one of her daughter's plays. Both parents were keen amateur players and Ngaio said in her autobiography *Black Beech and Honeydew*

(1965) that "there was almost always a play toward in our small family" (1). Ngaio joined in and not only learned basic stagecraft but also accompanied her mother to see traveling professional companies who managed to find their way to the theatre in Christchurch. The memory of Allan Wilkie's *Hamlet* stayed with her always, and it became her favorite Shakespeare play, one that she produced and directed twice in later years.

After leaving St. Margaret's Ngaio entered Canterbury College School of Art in Christchurch, determined to be a painter: "there was no question of looking on art as a sort of obsessive hobby--it was everything" (2). At the College she worked steadily between 1915 and 1919, encased in a rigorous academic approach to painting that she was too lacking in confidence to confront. Her paintings remain stiff and formal while her sketches and more private drawings reveal a much more relaxed and individual style. Clearly Ngaio was too dominated by what was considered to be "correct" style ever to find a significant place as a painter, although all through the 1920's and 1930's she continued to paint and joined with other painters to form "The Group," then considered to represent rather an avant-garde departure on the Christchurch artistic scene. For several years the distinguished New Zealand painter Evelyn Page and her composer husband Frederick created an artistic focal point for the Christchurch creative world in their idyllically-situated house on the shores of Lyttleton Harbour. A few years ago, guided by Ngaio's lifelong friend, the indefatigable Sylvia Fox, then nearly ninety and, alas, no longer with us, I found this house. Sylvia enthusiastically urged us on as we drove up the twisting Dyers Pass Road, determined to get to her destination, taking no notice of signs that said Private--"Drive on!" commanded Sylvia. So we did, and found the house, as beautiful as a dream landscape.

Writing, painting, acting, and producing plays occupied Ngaio fully during her early twenties. After leaving art college she became a professional actor with the Allan Wilkie Shakespeare Company touring New Zealand. She joined another professional company the following year and this became her drama school. From it came not only a practical knowledge of the stage in all its aspects but also a genuine love of the actor's world. She expressed her feelings best in her early novel *Vintage Murder* (1937), when her series detective Roderick Alleyn studies an assortment of actors on an overnight train:

> There was something about these people that
> gave them a united front. Their very manner
> in this night train, rattling and roaring through
> a strange country, was different from the man-
> ner of other travelers. Dozing a little, he saw
> them in more antiquated trains, in stage-coaches,
> in wagons, afoot, wearing strange garments,
> carrying bundles, but always together (3).

Ngaio's acting tours were not forgotten, and she used these memories for many of her theatrical novels, looking on them as "a little cellar of experiences which would one day be served up as the table wines of detective cookery" (4).

It was during this decade that Ngaio became acquainted with the Rhodes family, who were to become an integral part of her life from then on. The Rhodes family owned large tracts of New Zealand, and Tahu Rhodes and his young wife Helen (Lord Plunket's eldest daughter) with their children came out to New Zealand to live on one of the family's sheep stations after the first world war. The contact had been made through amateur dramatics and Ngaio was swiftly drawn into the world of the Christchurch gentry.

When the Duke of York visited the Rhodes's estate in 1926, Ngaio joined in with preparations for an impromptu entertainment in his honor: "I can only suppose that he, too, was unmusical or that we were bad enough to be funny; I know that we were bad" (5). This family were later to become fictionalized in Ngaio's novel *Death of a Peer* (1940), published as *Surfeit of Lampreys* in the U. K., and the friendship endured throughout their lives. When the Rhodes returned to England, they asked Ngaio to visit them, and her first trip "home" was made in 1928, taking several months aboard an ancient steamer to chug around the Cape of Good Hope and steer north to new horizons.

While painting and producing plays in Christchurch in the 1920's, Ngaio had also done quite a lot of journalism for local papers. She had written articles, poems, and plays and had started a serious novel about New Zealand which she brought with her to England. She was also commissioned to send back travel articles to New Zealand newspapers which provided a modest income; Ngaio was already beginning to support herself as a writer. Immediately upon arrival, she was swept into the high society world of London before the Depression when the atmosphere was heady and young people danced all night at clubs and restaurants: "I got the tag end of a very ravished but very wonderful 1920's in London," said Ngaio of this time (6). There were trips to Paris and Monte Carlo, where she won money at roulette and bought a suit. Above all, the excitement of the London theatre opened out before her. Even as an old lady, on her last trip to London nearly fifty years later, that special mood of anticipation when the lights go down and the magic of the play takes over never left her.

Roderick Alleyn made his entrance into this fashionable milieu--well-tailored, handsome, exquisitely mannered, and very much the kind of escort that Ngaio herself liked best. His credentials were impeccable but as a serving policeman, not an amateur like Lord Peter Wimsey, he could be very businesslike indeed when it came to dealing with the upper classes. Through her friendship with the Rhodes family and her entree into that aristocratic world, Ngaio was well placed to observe and to produce the exact nuance of conversation and behavior at country house weekends and society balls. Her plunge into crime fiction was, she claimed, rather accidental. Ngaio had abandoned her New Zealand novel, but finding one wet weekend that she was at a loss for something to do, she decided, as have so many other writers, that she could write a book as good or better than the "tec" she had been reading. Roderick Alleyn was initially entrusted to the pages of a penny exercise book and endured with surprising longevity throughout all the novels. His pursuit and marriage of Agatha Troy, the successful painter, ("The Siege of Troy," he calls it) underlie several novels in the late 1930's and introduce, perhaps, a little wish fulfillment on the part of their creator.

A Man Lay Dead (1934) was left with an agent when Ngaio returned hastily to New Zealand in 1932 after spending four invigorating years in England. Her mother was dying, and Ngaio spent the next sixteen years looking after her widowed father in Marton Cottage, the house that he had built for them at the beginning of the century. Ngaio's future as a novelist was established soon after her return, when her first book was published in 1934 by Geoffrey Bles and a contract was offered for other titles. At the age of forty she settled down to write, using all the experiences that she had carefully stored away. *Enter a Murderer* (1935) drew on her theatrical knowledge, as did *Vintage Murder* (1937). *The Nursing Home Murder* (1935), one of her most popular novels, drew on her friendship with a distinguished surgeon and memories of her own medical history. *Death in Ecstasy* (1936) arose in part from a scandal in Christchurch which she disguised with an English setting.   In 1937 she returned to Europe for an extended visit and this gave her the material for enough novels to keep her going for some time. *Artists in Crime* (1938), *Death in a White Tie* (1938), *Overture to Death* (1939), *Death at the Bar* (1940), *Death of a Peer* (1940), and *Death and the Dancing Footman* (1941) established her firmly as one of the most creative and inventive of contemporary crime novelists. Her sense of humor, her memorable characters, and her ingenious plots brought her a large readership in Britain, the United States, and around the world.   With Agatha Christie, Margery Allingham, and Dorothy L. Sayers she had been awarded the accolade of being one of the Queens of Crime.

From the 1930's onward Ngaio was represented by the agent Edmund Cork of Hughes Massie, whom she adored. Edmund was a perfect gentleman who knew exactly how to build up Ngaio's confidence and to introduce her to the London literary world. Before he died, I was fortunate to be able to talk to Edmund about his long friendship with Ngaio, which had clearly meant a great deal to them both. "I don't think I've ever known an author so humble," he told me, after a career in which he had dealt with a number of famous writers.   Edmund brought Ngaio to the Detection Club in 1937 when E. C. Bentley was installed as president, and she was highly entertained by the theatricality of the events:

> Mr. Bentley took the oath, John Rhode switched
> on the skull, Freeman Wills Crofts, who looked
> like a highly respected family solicitor, rather
> gingerly flourished the Sword, Anthony Gilbert
> displayed the Phial, and Miss Sayers, taking
> Edmund and me completely off our guard,
> loosed off her gun. The noise was deafening.

> I think I let out a yelp and I am sorry to
> record that dear Edmund, who has a loud
> laugh, laughed excessively (7).

The years of World War II were stark and dreary in New Zealand. Nearly 140,000 people (ten percent of the population) served overseas, but only after the fall of Singapore in 1942 did it become apparent that New Zealand and Australia could be open to invasion. Realizing that she was destined to forgo any trips to Europe for some time, Ngaio set her next two novels, *Colour Scheme* (1943) and *Died in the Wool* (1945), in New Zealand. Not only do they reveal her love of the New Zealand landscape, but they also display all her latent resistance to New Zealand accents and her admiration for English society, even when it is transplanted 12,000 miles. *Colour Scheme* was one of her own favorite novels and its murder weapon, a boiling mud pool, must be one of the most unusual in the history of the genre. What is fascinating in *Colour Scheme* is the way that she establishes the conventional country house mystery formula in a battered wooden guest house on the edge of the thermal area, while the murder investigation at the heart of *Died in the Wool* unfolds at an isolated sheep station high in the Southern Alps. Ngaio had first-hand knowledge of both these landscapes and her descriptions are highly evocative, particularly of the clear cold spaces of the high plateaus where she often painted on her expeditions into the mountains.

During World War II Ngaio drove an ambulance for the Red Cross, transporting wounded servicemen from the ports to hospitals. Fiercely patriotic, she almost wished that she could be in England to share in the struggle. She devised entertainments for convalescent soldiers and was much in demand as a producer for various amateur repertory societies. And, as a result of a commission from her new publisher,

William Collins, she wrote a short book (with the historian R. M. Burdon) about New Zealand for their British Commonwealth Picture series. Two of her own paintings are among the illustrations in this book, which clearly reveals the writer's love of her native land:

> The beaten track of tourists is not altogether the best track, and the unique landscapes of New Zealand lie a little away off it. Our thermal regions are probably less impressive than those of Yellowstone Park; our Alpine views lack the pretty floral foregrounds and charming chalets of the Austrian Tyrol and Switzerland. But Pohutokawa trees grow above bays of enchantment only in New Zealand, and nowhere else have I found any equivalent to the clear spaciousness of our mountain plateaux, or heard bird song as deep and moving as that of the New Zealand bush. This is a country so young that it impinges on the very ancient, and its clear and primordial landscape reaches back to emotions that have nothing to do with civilisation, but its spell-- once felt--is not easily forgotten (8).

The war years were also the period which saw Ngaio starting to create what has been called "The Golden Age" of New Zealand theatre. Working with students from Canterbury University College, but augmenting the student actors with seasoned amateur players and enhancing the productions with specially commissioned music, Ngaio embarked on a series of Shakespeare productions that was to span thirty years, from *Hamlet* in 1943 to *Henry V* in 1972. Her work with the students would result in triumphant tours

of New Zealand and Australia, and, over the years, a steady
flow of young actors trained by her would make their way into
the professional theatre and film world in the United States
and Britain. The film star Sam Neil played Theseus in her
1969 production of *A Midsummer Night's Dream,* and the
film director John Schlesinger acted in her 1951 *Twelfth
Night.* James Laurenson, her 1962 Macbeth, is now with the
Royal National Theatre in London; Jack Henderson worked
for the BBC; and Jonathan Elsom became well known as an
actor for his role in the "Crown Court" television series.
Lauris Edmond, who was in the first Shakespeare productions,
is a well known New Zealand writer. Many other student
players came over to Britain and returned to New Zealand to
set up other companies and to contribute to the artistic and
cultural growth of this new country; Elric Hooper has been
Artistic Director of the Court Theatre in Christchurch for
many years. Although Ngaio was always keen to encourage
young people to make their way to Europe and to train and to
establish standards, she also felt strongly that they should then
bring their talents back to New Zealand. Some of them did,
but not until the 1960's did professional theatre become firmly
established in the major cities. Until then the Marsh
productions in Christchurch continued to set standards of
excellence which often had touring professional companies
adversely compared to the native product.

In 1948 Ngaio Marsh was awarded the OBE (Order of
the British Empire) for services to literature and theatre in
New Zealand. She received the award from the Governor-
General in time to share the honor with her father, who was
then very frail. He died shortly afterwards and Ngaio, at the
age of fifty-three, was at liberty to take up a number of
opportunities as a writer and as a theatre producer. The next
few years were to see her established as an internationally
known figure in both spheres.

The novels written in the late 1940's, *Final Curtain* (1947) and *Swing, Brother, Swing* (1949)--published as *A Wreath for Rivera* in the U. S. --both reveal the effects of the author's distance from English society. The exhausted nation was then creeping slowly back towards prosperity after the damage and privations of the second world war, and was very different from the country she had last visited ten years before. Ngaio was desperate to return, and in 1949 she embarked on an extended visit to England. She returned as a celebrated detective fiction writer and a confident theatre director. Penguin, in association with Collins, published the "Marsh Million" at the end of July, issuing 100,000 copies of ten novels accompanied by a great deal of publicity. Ngaio became much in demand as a broadcaster on BBC Radio, where her attractive deep voice, ready store of Shakespearean quotations, and dry sense of humor made her a popular figure for quiz shows and talks. Ngaio accepted the part she was to play as though it had been presented in a bound script. She rented a flat in a fashionable part of London. She walked a Siamese cat on a jewelled lead. She purchased a costly Jaguar car which she drove with panache around London and down to Kent to see her friends, the Rhodes family. In town she dressed from Harrods and Hardy Amies. With her height (she was 5' 10" tall) and her striking face, she wore hats well and heads would turn when she entered a room. Despite this glamorous protective layer she was often desperately shy, and still rather overpowered by the London literary set.

The two years that Ngaio spent in London from 1949 to 1951 represented a pivotal point in her life. One of her novels, *Surfeit of Lampreys*, was dramatized and performed at the Embassy Theatre, Hampstead. And Ngaio herself was invited to direct a production of Pirandello's *Six Characters in Search of an Author*, one of her favorite plays. She may have been directing on the fringe, but it was still in the London professional theatre, and the reviews were almost all very favorable. Ngaio was asked to direct a season of English comedy at the Embassy Theatre for Festival of Britain Year, 1951. On the face of it, the offer would seem to represent everything that Ngaio relished--a chance to stay longer in Britain, and to be part of a world that she found unfailingly stimulating. What could possibly be set against this to cause her to decline?

The significance of the British Commonwealth had always been important to Ngaio, and she often spoke in public about the importance of retaining links between countries that were grouped under its banner. When she was asked to create a British Commonwealth Theatre Company, composed of actors from many countries to tour all over the world, she could not resist. The decision took her first to Australia and then back to New Zealand and to her roots in Christchurch. The tour was a disaster and its grandiose aspirations foundered on the level of practical problems. A high point in Ngaio's life had been reached in London, but the low point, with empty theatres and a disgruntled company, was very low indeed. It took her some time to recover from the disappointment of this misguided enterprise.

From this point on, Ngaio's life fell into a comfortable pattern. She continued to live in the family home on the Cashmere Hills, spending about nine months to write a novel and devoting the rest of the year to producing and directing a Shakespeare play with a large cast of students. Her reputation within New Zealand grew, and students who worked with her regarded it as a privilege, if a very demanding one. At one stage in my research I wondered if it was possible to meet any New Zealander who had not either acted in a Ngaio Marsh production or whose parents had not done so. This is the reason why, in New Zealand, Ngaio Marsh is known for her work in the theatre, not for her literary achievements.

This was also the stage where my interviews as a biographer began to add the detail to Ngaio as a person. Few people remembered her during the 1920's or 1930's, and she herself left very little written material, apart from the highly selective accounts of her early years in *Black Beech and Honeydew.* But the students with whom she worked in Christchurch in the 1940's remember vividly the effect that she had on them. Many of them told me of the special magic that she gave to their lives, and they have never forgotten those exciting, highly-charged days. Not only impressionable students, but other creative artists gathered around the focus provided by the Little Theatre. Douglas Lilburn, now a highly respected New Zealand composer, wrote incidental music for her early productions. Craftsmen at the Caxton Press produced finely printed theatre programs, and for many years Ngaio personally signed all the first night programs.

By this time, Ngaio was receiving a very satisfactory income from her writing. Novels were being translated and published around the world, with especially strong markets in the United States. Serial versions of novels printed in magazines brought her to an even wider public. She was able to employ help in the house and to entertain visitors to Christchurch (such as Joyce Grenfell, J. B. Priestley and Jacquetta Hawkes) with considerable style. She turned Marton Cottage into a southern hemisphere replica of an English country house and garden, with expensive chintz curtains brought back from England, antique furniture and floral arrangements. A mural of "The Tempest" was painted over the fireplace in the drawing room, and many other fascinating theatrical mementos were displayed. The garden was filled with terraces of roses but native flowers and shrubs were also cherished, including the little white flowered ngaio shrub after which she was named.

Here she would sit in her armchair (never at a desk), writing page after page of virtually seamless manuscript on ruled foolscap paper. Her hand written manuscripts are mainly held by the Alexander Turnbull Library in Wellington, New Zealand, but some are preserved by the Mugar Library in Boston, Massachusetts. Virtually all reveal remarkable fluency in the development of the novels, with very few alterations. For a long time she cherished an old Conway Stewart fountain pen, using green ink. Then she began to use ball point, and sometimes even felt pen. A great joy presents itself for the snooping biographer in finding around the margins of the pages little sketches of her cats, or the characters that she was writing about, or perhaps, if her mind wandered too far, a drawing of a stage set for one of her forthcoming productions. Just occasionally a grocery list or a seating plan for a dinner party slip in. Every Christmas she entertained the children of her friends to an elaborate "Christmas Tree Party" when she tried to create the atmosphere of an English country house with church bells and carols echoing out into the hot Christchurch summer. She gave lavish presents to all her guests, many of them collected during her trips overseas and brought back in huge property baskets. Ngaio herself always spent Christmas on her own, reluctant to impose herself on even her closest friends.

As Ngaio grew older, her energy appeared to be unfailing, although she did admit to needing regular infusions of what she called "that London feeling"--the surge of excitement that inevitably came to her when she was living in the heart of the city that she loved. She made further lengthy visits to England during the next twenty years, her last being in 1974. Ngaio refused to fly, and the era of the great ocean liners was coming to an end. Ending, too, was all the theatrical glamor of first class travel, dressing for dinner, eating at the captain's table and surveying a fascinating assortment of fellow guests. She thoroughly enjoyed these leisurely voyages and generally used them to work without interruption on a novel. Occasionally she would bring a secretary with her to keep up with the typing. It was on one of these ocean liners that an elderly lady deferentially approached Ngaio where she sat in a corner of the upper deck and asked in all seriousness if the author always knew who the murderer was. Ngaio was able to assure her, again with perfect gravity, that writers nearly always had this worked out before they began. Given the intricacy of Ngaio's plots, it is very difficult to assume otherwise, and her few surviving notes for various finished novels reveal substantial preparation before she began to write. Always character was to lead these plots: "I invariably start with people," she said (9), and her talent for characterization could sometimes create tension between the detective element and the wider dimensions of the plot.

Ngaio's role as a public figure became well established during the 1960's. She visited Japan and the United States as part of a lengthy voyage back to England in 1960. In both countries she was highly acclaimed. After landing in San Francisco and speaking to various groups of admirers there ("such hats!"), she traveled across the continent by train, arriving in New York to find herself treated like a celebrity. Her packed schedule included literary lunches and interviews by editors from the *New York Times, Newsweek,* and the *New York Herald Tribune.* Fortunately for Ngaio it also gave her time to renew her acquaintance with her American agent, Dorothy Olding, of Harold Ober Associates. They had previously met in London and Dorothy's dry wit was entirely on Ngaio's wave length. Not only that, she was a helpful companion in an unfamiliar environment (although she was slightly startled by Ngaio's requests to visit Greenwich Village at night and to walk in Central Park), and their subsequent friendship was maintained through many meetings and partings.

The next two years were happily spent in London writing the first draft of her autobiography, *Black Beech and Honeydew* (1965), continuing with her twenty-second novel, *Hand in Glove* (1962), and working on a theatrical version of her novel *False Scent* for professional performance in Worthing late in 1961. She bought a new Jaguar, this time a black XK150 sports car, and after using it for tootling around London (to the theatre, or to Harrods for the lamb chops), had it shipped back to New Zealand where it became the most famous car on the South Island. Ngaio drove it, very fast, until she was over eighty and cataracts finally prevented her from taking it out. Stories about the car and its dashing driver are legendary in Christchurch. Once at the University she ran over a bicycle and amazed the owner by immediately presenting him with name and address on a card: "Just take it to this chap to be mended, will you? I always have them sent there."

The snobbish high culture attitude of the New Zealand academic world--which had always made Ngaio feel rather defensive about her detective novels--was finally broached in 1962 when the University of Canterbury at Christchurch, having been made an independent institution the previous year, awarded her the honorary degree of Doctor of Literature. The Public Orator praised her contribution to New Zealand culture: her "diligent application, her craftsmanship and inventiveness which enabled her to publish one book a year." She was especially thanked for her work with the Drama Society. Ngaio wore her scarlet robes and grey hood with a flourish--"no-one had ever worn academic dress quite like Ngaio Marsh," remarked a member of staff. A few months earlier she had delivered the Macmillan Brown Lectures at the University, a prestigious lecture series which summarized all the wisdom achieved after a lifetime spent as a lover of theatre. They were called "The Three-Cornered World: Shakespeare in the Theatre," and focused on the contribution of the producer, the actor, and the audience.

During 1962 Ngaio was deeply involved in working with the New Zealand composer David Farquhar in creating the opera "A Unicorn for Christmas" which was based on her children's play, "The Wyvern and the Unicorn." The opera built up a vast momentum, culminating in a performance before Her Majesty the Queen and the Duke of Edinburgh in Auckland on 7 February 1963, when Ngaio was presented to the royal visitors. What was being called "the first New Zealand opera" caused a great deal of controversy, with its Eurocentric leanings not being entirely acceptable at a time when consciousness of New Zealand's cultural independence was growing. There is no doubt, however, that the award of the DBE (Dame Commander, Order of the British Empire) to Ngaio in 1966 was a source of great pride to most New Zealanders. The following year she opened the new Ngaio Marsh Theatre in the University of Canterbury with her own production of *Twelfth Night*.

The role of public figure, into which Ngaio was now propelled, was time-consuming and it was hardly surprising that writing the annual detective novel was occasionally proving difficult. Lengthy stays in England provided not only inspiration for new plots, but also uninterrupted writing time. Proximity to her raw material always produced her finest novels, and the work done in the 1950's and 1960's is certainly and liveliest and best fiction. Her last trip to England was in 1974, and it was prolonged by a serious operation for cancer. When she finally returned to her own house and garden the following year, she knew that she had visited England for the last time. Her friends thought that she was remarkable at the age of seventy-six; in fact, she was now over eighty, and still writing as professionally as she ever had done.

Ngaio's health deteriorated during the next few years, with angina, failing sight, and deafness, but she still kept writing. On two occasions newspapers around the world falsely reported her death in a Christchurch hospital. She now had a living-in housekeeper to look after her, and was supported by a close and devoted circle of friends who not only helped her to look after her daily routine, but wisely recognized that it was crucial to arrange lifts so that Ngaio could keep attending the theater. Even though frail health was beginning to narrow her world, she was not forgotten as a writer. She was delighted when in 1978 the Mystery Writers of America made her a Grand Master and gave her their much coveted Edgar Award, a small ceramic statuette of Edgar Allan Poe. The invitation to attend the ceremony in Los Angeles, reluctantly, had to be declined. She had been earlier recognized by the British Crime Writers Association in 1955 with their Red Herrings Award for *Scales of Justice*.

On 23 April 1979, Collins sent bouquets of flowers and celebratory telegrams for Ngaio's supposed eightieth birthday. Even Ngaio admitted to some embarrassment at this point. Curiously, she did not seem to realize that her advanced years were a source of great admiration for those who knew her, and the fact that at the age of eighty-four she was still able to write a sparkling and unusual novel such as *Photo Finish* (1980), with no apparent diminution in style or vigor is astonishing. She laid down her pen six weeks before she died, having completed her final novel, *Light Thickens* (1982), still hand written on fine lined paper, and, if not one of her strongest plots, still containing marvelous insights into Shakespearean production and the theater world.

The life of Ngaio Marsh was full of achievement, yet the more I came to know her, the more I felt that it also contained much sadness. She was passionately supportive of

New Zealand artists and groups, maintaining always that only the highest standards should be striven for in any of the arts. This was her public side. Her private emotions were seldom allowed to show. Every life has its greetings and farewells, yet for Ngaio the many partings that characterized her journeys to and from Europe were often very difficult to bear. She never married, and increasingly found deep friendships among her young actors and with her two second cousins, John and "Bear" Mannings. They responded to her sympathetic understanding, but often did not realize her own vulnerability. Only in retrospect, with the benefit of their own maturity, did they realize how lonely she was.

In Ngaio's theatre productions she always searched for "a touch of magic" to surprise and delight her audience. In her life, too, that touch of magic reached many people, and their lives changed as a result. Please forgive me for concluding with a quotation from my own book:

> Writing to friends just before she died, about
> her last novel, *Light Thickens*, and the profound
> uncertainties that she felt about the manuscript,
> she concluded characteristically, "I'm glad I tried."
> What better epitaph could anyone request?
> Except, perhaps, the words of the late Sir
> Anthony Quayle, actor, director and a friend for
> many years, who wrote about Ngaio, "She was a
> generous, intelligent, warm-hearted spirit and
> made the world a richer place" (10).

ENDNOTES

1. Ngaio Marsh, *Black Beach and Honeydew* (Boston: Little, Brown and Company, 1965), 27; hereafter cited as *BBHD*.
2. Marsh, *BBHD*, 111.
3. Ngaio Marsh, *Vintage Murder* (New York: Jove Books, 1978), 14.
4. Marsh, *BBHD*, 182.
5. Marsh, *BBHD*, 201.
6. Ngaio Marsh, interview New Zealand Radio, 22 August 1954.
7. Marsh, *BBHD*, rev. ed. (Auckland: Fontana/Collins, 1981), 307.
8. Ngaio Marsh (with R. M. Burdon), *New Zealand* (London: Collins, 1942), 47.
9. Ngaio Marsh, Marsh papers, Alexander Turnbull Library, Wellington, N. Z.
10. Margaret Lewis, *Ngaio Marsh: A Life* (London & New Zealand: Chatto & Windus, 1991), x.

Thoughts on the Life of a Marvelous Woman

by John Dacres-Mannings

The public image of Ngaio Marsh is that of a fine writer, an authority on Shakespeare, and a competent painter. But her greatness lay not in these areas--it lay in a magic personality. I have met many major figures in the arts, politics, and the military. None has had the compelling magnetism which surrounded Dame Ngaio. It was perhaps this magnetism which enabled me to move into her orbit with such ease and parental acceptance. Yet she was never aware that she had this remarkable quality. This judgment is not entirely a subjective perception. For example, those very few people who were close to her, including my mother and others outside the family, find themselves saying to themselves, as I still do now ten years after her death, "I must tell Ngaio about this." I have known some even go to the telephone to ring her. She was a remarkable woman.

In a crowded room, there was always a flock of people wishing to meet her and hoping to talk to her. Not about her writing. Not about the theatre. Just to talk to her. I meet many people now who, knowing the relationship, come up and say, "I met Dame Ngaio once. What a marvelous woman she was." The words are often repeated. Again, this grew not out of the theatre, nor out of her writing, for many were interested in neither. Nor was it because she was a public figure. It was a strange spell that she cast seemingly without being aware of the fact.

Dame Ngaio was a striking looking woman, tall and impressive. When she entered a room, everyone stopped talking and looked at her. It used to embarrass me as a child. When she needed to go out, she would wear large pieces of costume jewelry. They always looked right and this added to her presence.

Furs were her passion. Furs and fine Georgian crystal. The latter regularly was broken by housekeepers. Curiously, she was little interested in silver or elaborate jewelry. My own family had a substantial amount of inherited silver and I was brought up to love and revere it. The Marsh family silver went down a different family branch. She took no interest in replacing it. The silver she did have was of fine quality and rivalled much of my own.

Dame Ngaio was my mother's first cousin, making me her first cousin once removed. We met in New Zealand shortly before World War II broke out when I was perhaps six or seven. We fell greatly in love and remained so until her death, and for me, indeed, beyond. Our characters were unusually similar in many ways. She was perhaps the only person with whom I could carry on a conversation without speaking. There was a sort of telepathy between us. I did not see a lot of her despite the bond that existed between us until I went to school at Christ's College.

During my school days in Christchurch, our relationship blossomed. Each Sunday after Communion and Matins, we boys were allowed out to specified homes. Mine was Dame Ngaio's. Each Sunday I would ride my bicycle to Dame Ngaio's home and spend the hours available working in the garden, which I loved, or playing classical music, or talking to Dame Ngaio. On weekdays during the holidays mid-morning we had "elevenses"--usually a glass of Madeira and cheese and biscuits.

On Sundays precisely at 10:30 AM two very elderly family friends, James and Cecil Walker, arrived for coffee. Both bachelors, they came from an old English family which had brought out to New Zealand a very large quantity of silver, fine furniture, and paintings. James, the elder brother, had been a ballet dancer and actor in his youth, which was not thought to be appropriate for a gentleman in his generation. He was a mine of information and discussed London and local theatre, actors and actresses of yesteryear and the current day. He was a great outlet for Dame Ngaio's fascination with the theatre. The other brother, Cecil, had trained as an engineer but never practiced. He would talk to my uncle and me, while Dame Ngaio and James discussed the theatre and the arts generally. At precisely one o'clock they left, only to arrive again in the evening. They came to play Lexicon (much like today's Scrabble), in which I joined if I was not at school. It was all very formal, and few words were uttered.

Lunch was served each day by Crawsie, Dame Ngaio's cook/housekeeper, a remarkable Irish woman renowned for her malapropisms. "Panklets" were one of her specialities. Fortunately, not enamored with pancakes, I was spared this ultimate reward. For lunch we had wine or a fine but powerful New Zealand cider. I had my own room and would often go to it and play records or potter around the garden while Dame Ngaio had an afternoon sleep. In the evening, on the grounds that school boys are always underfed, a large meal--preceded by brandy and soda and accompanied by wine or cider--was prepared by Crawsie. Trifle heavily soaked in brandy was the usual pudding thought appropriate for a half-starved school boy. (We were in fact well fed at school.) Somewhat unsteady, I would pedal back to school, Evensong, Compline, and bed.

Dame Ngaio had a rapport with children equalled by few I have known. At any gathering children flocked to her, abandoning their parents and playmates. She had the capacity to think with a child's mind. At her funeral, a friend who had known her all his life mentioned to me that as a child he always thought her to be the same age as he was. Her personality was so powerful that differences of height and voice evaporated. I recall when I was very young her asking my advice about buying a camera. With great seriousness, we had the stock of a camera shop examined. I was most proud to have had my advice sought on such a matter. After much thought and discussion as to the merits of each, I suggested one which she bought. And handed to me. She understood children.

We boys were allowed two theatre or cinema leaves a term. These were great occasions. Dame Ngaio and I had dinner with lots of food, and two or three helpings of ice cream. A huge box of chocolates always accompanied these events, so large that one marched back to school with most of the box intact.

When children went to England by air, the only destination for New Zealanders in those days, she would give each of the children a number of presents--one to be opened in Singapore, one at the next refueling station, and so on until they arrived in London. She loved children, but I suspect on the whole may not have enjoyed having children permanently around her.

She herself hated traveling by air. And curiously enough, the planes seemed to resent her dislike. On the few occasions she went by air, because of the phasing out of liners, fate always took a hand. Engines would fall out and the plane would be grounded. Coming to Sydney for my son Nicholas's Confirmation provided one desperate attempt to come to terms with modern technology. Record snow fell on the Christchurch airfield. She was shunted back and forth for three days from her home to the airport while men tried to remove snow faster than it fell. One serious attempt to rectify the lapsed timetable resulted in a plane lumbering down the runway like a great seal seeking to become airborne, only to plough into a drift of snow and stop. She did in fact make it on time, then able to prove beyond all doubt the old adage that if God wanted men to fly.... It was difficult to argue against her crushing if unusual theological logic.

When in New Zealand, as she was for most of my school days, she took control of the Canterbury University Drama Society and produced Shakespeare plays. It became her fiefdom when she was in New Zealand. It faded away when she was not there. This absorbed a great deal of her time. Those students who had ability found some way of remaining attached to the University, so that when she would arrive back in New Zealand, she thus had a permanent core of well trained students to take the more difficult parts. Rehearsals took place in any accommodation which was cheap--a rowing shed, a disused malt house. On some occasions she was able to have the use of suitable quarters at the University. They all had one characteristic--they were cold. Oil heaters were brought in, but the high ceilings prevented any material effect. She would wrap herself in a large fur, a new one nearly always accompanying her on her return from England, the old one usually being given to the secretary of the day.

From time to time she would consult me about minor matters relating to a play she was producing. Sitting in a large, deep armchair working out the moves for a production of *Antony and Cleopatra*, she looked up over her large glasses and asked, "John, how old do you think Cleopatra should be?" At my age then, sex up to the age of twenty-five was romantic. Sex over the age of twenty-five was disgusting. I quickly answered, "No more than twenty-five." Half to herself she said, "Mmmm. She was of course forty-eight," and then went back to her big promptbook. She had to choose between two good actresses, one in her early twenties and one much older. The younger one got the part.

Dame Ngaio was a very private person. In Christchurch she seldom accepted invitations, and seldom had her friends to dinner. When she did entertain either in New Zealand or in London, they were splendid affairs. There was a ritual, however, to solve the lack of general hospitality. Usually once a year she had a cocktail party. Perhaps eighty or a hundred people would attend. Indeed people would come, if necessary, on crutches or in a wheel chair. Her formula seldom changed. White Lady cocktails were served at nearly full strength--which of course was nearly raw alcohol--on the grounds that guests became more relaxed. Once a couple of glasses had been consumed, the cocktail was diluted significantly. On one occasion my brother, who was visiting, and I forgot our instructions. Near to neat alcohol in the undiluted White Ladies was consumed in great quantities with predictable results. One guest fell to the floor asleep. No one seemed to notice. A former head of the Imperial Indian Police was unable to get out of his chair, muttering, "And me a church warden!"

Not all parties turned into alcoholic orgies. Dame Ngaio did entertain to dinner many leading figures. As the man of her house, I met and in some cases came to know many interesting people who would come to dinner. People like Sir Laurence Olivier and Lady Olivier (Vivien Leigh), the Shakespearean actor Anthony Quayle who served with great distinction in MI6 in Albania, Sir Robert Helpmann the dancer, Dame Marie Rambert the ballet producer, Sir William Collins the publisher, and distinguished concert pianists and conductors as well as British generals and governors general. As a little boy, I found the dinner parties awesome. The conversation might be about a new production of a

Shakespearean play, a Chekhov play, or about Dostoyevski, Puccini, or a spectacular production of an opera at Covent Garden or a ballet about which I knew nothing. If there were generals present, it might be about war episodes which I was too young to remember and had not yet learned about. It was a little difficult for me at that age to sit at the head of the table and enter into intelligent conversation at the level which abounded. It provided me, however, with an awareness that out there, yet to be discovered, was a world of magic waiting for me.

Dame Ngaio took my upbringing very seriously. She was never quite sure how to do it, but was determined to do it well. She took great pains to ensure that I was brought up a Gentleman. They existed in those days. My sex education presented something of a problem. The only child of her parents, unmarried, and without the benefit of any love affairs of which I am aware,   she was under some handicap. Nevertheless, she set about it with a will.   Undaunted, she scoured material from any gynaecologist she knew. Large volumes of specialist material concerning the female anatomy used to appear silently upon my dressing table only to disappear with equal mysteriousness a week or two later to be replaced by a new volume of medical intelligence. As a high church Anglican, she also took a keen interest in my religious life, and yet was never quite able to recover the faith she had as a child. It was one of her great regrets. She suffered much spiritual torment and greatly envied those who had a less difficult path on which to travel. On such matters as wine and food, and the protocols of the upper classes, she was on much firmer ground, making it easy for me when, having left school after the war, I went to England and into the British Army.

Her great love, of course, was England, where she spent much of her early adult life and many of her later years. And yet she loved New Zealand, in particular Christchurch and her home, which was very dear to her and to me. When I went into the British Army, her father having died, she followed me to London and took a house. I was then what was called a Gentleman Cadet training for a commission in the Royal Artillery, which had been my family's principal regiment. Our training was severe. We spent some hours most days on the parade ground, being shouted at by sergeant majors from the Grenadier Guards and the Coldstream Guards.

Numerous times a junior sergeant major would approach the senior sergeant major bashing us around the parade ground and at a suitable opportunity would hand him a telegram. "Mr. Dacres-Mannings, Sir. Please fall out." He would hand me the telegram. "I am sorry, Sir. You are excused the rest of the parade." Dame Ngaio did not like writing letters on the whole. Writing was her profession. Whenever possible she would send telegrams. I would open the telegram and read, "I thought it might be fun if we went to Paris for the weekend. I have booked rooms at the George Cinq." And then would follow the details. The sergeant majors would be kind to me for the rest of the day. That the telegrams came rather frequently must have suggested that I had a very large family, and that longevity was not a family trait.

Normal weekend leaves were spent with Dame Ngaio at her house in London. One, which she had for some years, was in Hans Road opposite Harrods the great London department store. It made shopping very easy. It was close to numerous restaurants which solved the problem of meals when there was no one to cook for us. She and I enjoyed each other's company enormously, and on the whole there was not much time to be diverted to a lot of social activity. There were cocktail parties, where again White Ladies were served, these times on a more controlled basis. As in New Zealand an invitation was always accepted, and one met senior men from Scotland Yard, leading literary and theatre people, and members of our English family.

London is a vibrant city. There is so much to see, and do, and love. One could spend a lifetime and still so much would be new. We would walk along famous streets and see the Monopoly board come to life. Go to Kensington Garden where Peter Pan lives. Go to Baker Street on the chance of meeting Sherlock Holmes or Dr. Watson. Pass a stone laid by Sir Richard Whittington, Lord Mayor of London, but without mention of his cat. Visit the Victoria and Albert Museum and marvel at the beautiful pieces displayed there. The Old Bailey produced detective novels in the flesh and remained a continuous source of interest and spectacle. Then we would have lunch at a restaurant and pursue our quests. In the evening we would go to a play, a concert, the opera, or the ballet, and thence to dinner. Some weekends we would go and stay with the family. While they were very dear to us, and for me remain so, we both loved London best.

What can I say about her writing? Sadly, very little. She used to write late at night and into the early hours of the morning. She wrote about upper class English life, about which she was fully conversant. She had much difficulty embracing the changes which took place during and after the war. To me, having been in New Zealand during the war, the scale of life in England was, and still is, magical. To her it was a shadow of what had been her life for the many years she lived in England. To a considerable extent hers was a prewar England, and this sometimes gives her writing something of an old world quality. Perhaps in her writing she could relive those very happy earlier days.

At times I used to encourage the possibility of writing a non-detective novel. Her style, perception, and skill--it seemed to me--would have the capacity to produce novels of a very high standard. The difficulty, she would point out, was that her name was permanently fixed in the public mind on detective story writing. When a reader sees a book, he knows it will be a detective story. If it were a standard novel, he would feel tricked. We discussed writing under a pseudonym. She felt that it would be too great a job to establish a new name, particularly as her own was so well known and her formula successful. I've often thought she should have tried.

She did not enjoy writing but writing provided the wherewithal to support a fairly comfortable life style, and more particularly when she was in New Zealand, the financing of Shakespearean plays which she produced. In view of the small population of Christchuch, these were not always a commercial success despite the very high standard she achieved. She felt embarrassed that she wrote, thinking--I suspect--that detective story writing was a long way from Shakespeare, her God.

As Dr. Margaret Lewis has pointed out, none of Dame Ngaio's close family or friends were detective fiction readers. There is no-one who was close to Dame Ngaio who would be able to speak about her writing. Her private life and her life as a writer were two separate compartments. A third compartment was the theatre. The compartments were seldom combined. That is why people who feel they knew her well will say that their association was limited merely to one facet of a giant personality. Dr. Lewis also commented that this made it very difficult to write Dame Ngaio's biography.
I have always believed that the fact that so few of her close relations ever took a keen interest in her writing may have been that her personality was so great that writing and even the theatre were of minor importance by comparison. She was a person ten feet tall, quite the most magical person I have ever known. Once one starts thinking about her even now, it is almost impossible to stop. I still miss her greatly.

Outsold and Outsmarted, But...

by H. R. F. Keating

I first met Ngaio Marsh in person in 1974--I had known her through Inspector Alleyn, my feet in his shoes, since I was barely a teenager--when with Julian Symons we were sent by Collins Crime Club on a short publicity tour to Yorkshire. So my first recollection of her really, is of sitting at a table next to hers with a small pile of my books at my elbow and watching her, with several toppling piles of her books at her elbow, signing and signing away for the guests, mostly behatted, at the *Yorkshire Post* Literary Luncheon where we had all three spoken. I seem to remember that the long winding comet-tail waiting to come to her occasionally sent off a single desperate spark in my direction.

But, by then having shared a compartment in the train up from London with her, I could not find it in my heart to be jealous of a person so beamingly and simply friendly.

And worse was to come at the end of that short tour. Going back on the train, with Ngaio dropping out of the conversation from time to time briskly to deal with *The Times* crossword, Julian mentioned that he was engaged on a book with as hero, or as flawed a hero as he ever puts into his books, an actor who had got more or less taken over by the Sherlock Holmes figure he had long played on television. But, he said, he had so far failed to bring to mind an appropriate Holmesian dictum to use as the title. I had barely had time to register that here was a challenge when Ngaio without a moment's hesitation produced "A Three-pipe Problem." ("It is quite a three-pipe problem," Holmes remarks in "The Red-Headed League.") And that title the book bore, with a dedication to Ngaio, when it came out in 1975.

Again, I could bear no grudge. Especially when I thought of what we had been through together in those few fairly hectic days in Yorkshire. A visit, at Ngaio's particular insistence, of course, to Haworth to stand with her in that tiny no-fireplace room above the front door where--which one of the Brontës was it who slept and coughed away there? Certainly not Bramwell. But that was pleasure for all of us. No, the real ordeal came in breezy Scarborough.

It was a specially arranged Dickensian dinner at the hotel where we stayed. And grim. Beyond words. Serving wenches -- I'm sure they were anachronistically called that-- dressed to display maximum bosom. And when, striving for the politeness I felt Ngaio would expect of me, I asked the slim under-manager who it was who played Mr. Bumble, "I do" came the prompt and puling answer. I wish I could recall Ngaio standing up to the rigors of that evening. But merciful forgetfulness has descended.

Alas, that was the only time I met her. She fell seriously ill some months later and was unable to come to be, very belatedly, initiated into the Detection Club. And that visit to England was the last she made. But she did, in a way, come to us once more. It was in 1991, the year Margaret Lewis's fine biography came out. I was, by this time, President of the Detection Club and it occurred to me that at our Annual Dinner we ought to celebrate Ngaio's life and art.

It is a tradition in the Club occasionally to put on for the amusement of our members and their guests some sort of theatrical turn. In days gone by Dorothy L. Sayers had been a robust Mrs. Hudson in a Sherlockian romp written by John Dickson Carr, *The Case of the Ambassador's Trousers.* While in 1990, the centenary of Agatha Christie's birth, my wife, Sheila Mitchell, had played opposite Harold Pinter, Antonia Fraser's husband, in an excerpt from *Witness for the Prosecution.* So I managed to hammer out a sort of play from the early scenes of Ngaio's English village mystery *Overture to Death.* But the dramatic pistol shot that comes from within the piano as Miss Campanula planks down her foot on the soft pedal and launches into Rachmaninoff's *Prelude in C Sharp Minor* was beyond any resources the Club could summon up. Yet we triumphed. At that key moment from out of the darkness beyond our tiny stage came a voice.

> *The air was blown into splinters of atrocious clamour. For a second nothing existed but noise -- hard racketing noise. The hall, suddenly thick with dust, was also thick with a cloud of intolerable sound. And, as the dust fell, so the pandemonium abated and separated into recognizable sources. Women were screaming. Chair legs scraped the floor, branches of evergreens fell from the walls, the piano hummed like a gigantic top. Miss Campanula fell forward. Her face slid down the sheet of music, which stuck to it. Very slowly and stealthily she slipped sideways to the keys of the piano, striking a final discord in the bass. She remained there, quite still, in a posture that seemed to parody the antics of an affected virtuoso. She was dead.*

Was it that of our guest of honor, Margaret Lewis? Or was it Ngaio herself?

Random Recollections

by Julian Symons

All the notable women crime writers I've known have had some outstanding quality in their personalities. In Dorothy L. Sayers it was a magisterial intellect, in Agatha Christie an emotionally paralyzing shyness, in Margaret Millar an outspokenness that could seem like aggression until she laughed at her own outrageousness. P. D. James hides her sharp mind behind a natural exuberance of manner, Ruth Rendell and Patricia Highsmith give the impression of guarding secrets as subtle as those revealed in their books. The quality I associate with Ngaio Marsh is charm. She was not just beautiful and elegant, although those would be appropriate words. She had an ease of manner, and a real or apparent interest in a companion's conversation, that are very rare. They were combined with a curiously innocent excitement about anything going on around her that had an element of drama. I think she liked life to be theatrical, and indeed the theatre was her true love, her work as a stage producer what she most valued.

I didn't know her well--better by correspondence than in person--and although I hope and believe we were friendly, it would be wrong to claim I was a friend. She came to dinner once when we lived in the South London suburb of Blackheath, and fitted smoothly into a collection of strangers including her fellow crime writer John Bingham. Much later,

when she was in England on a brief visit, my wife and I went
to a party at which most of the guests were young people
connected with the theatre who obviously adored her.

My clearest recollection, though, is of a publisher-
sponsored trip she took with Harry Keating and me, at which
we talked about ourselves and our work to receptive
audiences in the Midlands and the North of England, ending
up in Scarborough. Ngaio was already suffering from heart
trouble and hesitated about making the trip, but as she said to
one audience, when she heard that "the great Panjandrum
himself, with the little round button at top" was going on it,
she knew she had to say yes. This was said in gentle mockery
of what she felt to be my too-frequent laying down of the law
about crime stories. She was not at all averse from gentle
mockery and on this occasion the listeners duly laughed,
although few of them are likely to have recognized the
quotation from Samuel Foote's eighteenth-century nonsense
verse.

She was a delightful companion on this trip and
enjoyed our visit to Haworth and the Brontë country, but
pleaded tiredness as a reason for abstention from celebratory
evenings. On our journey back in the train she suggested the
title for a book I'd almost finished about an actor playing
Sherlock Holmes on TV who becomes involved in trying to
solve a real crime by Sherlockian methods. "Why not call it a
three pipe problem?" she said. I did, and dedicated the book
to her.

A little while after that she took issue with remarks of
mine in *Bloody Murder* about her "taking refuge from real
emotional problems in the official investigation and
interrogation of suspects." This, she said, was "one of the
major limitations of the genre," and something she found it
impossible to get around. "I invariably start with people about

whom I would like to write," but then came the need to involve one of them in committing a violent crime. She came to the conclusion already reached by Raymond Chandler, that "the more deeply and honestly (an author) examines his characters, the more disquieting becomes the skulduggery that he is obliged to practise in respect to the guilty party." She was generous enough to say I had walked that tightrope successfully, along with Margery Allingham and Wilkie Collins--and I'm sure she would nowadays have added other names. But it was a tightrope she never attempted to walk herself, and although personally I regret that, it does emphasize the fact that what she was doing as an innovative New Zealand stage producer was more important to her than the books she wrote.

At the end of the 1970's I was gathering stories for the Detection Club anthology *Verdict of Thirteen* and asked Ngaio if she would write something for the collection. My letter was rather hesitant, knowing she was not well and did not find the short story an altogether congenial form. She replied saying something like "as it's you I suppose I shall have to try," and produced a short story that was certainly one of the best in the book. In the last letter I had from her, in 1979 three years before her death, she said she was very homesick for London, "but there are health difficulties nowadays" and her doctors said air travel was "a bit risky." Her last visit to England was in 1974. I wish I'd got to know her better.

Theatre in Life and Fiction

Ngaio Marsh: A Theatrical Avocation

by Paul R. Bushnell

It was more than just the opening of a play when the curtains parted for a production of *The Moon Princess* on the little raked stage of the St. Michael & All Angels Church hall on September 9th in 1913. Few in the Christchurch audience can have suspected that the writer and co-director of this fairy play, a precocious eighteen-year-old girl from a genteel middle-class family, had that night begun a theatrical career which would span six decades of New Zealand's theatre history.

Fifty-nine years later, Ngaio Marsh would direct her swansong Shakespearean play *Henry V,* setting the seal on a glittering career in the theatre. This production would be mounted in a spirit of civic celebration to mark the opening of a new theatre built as part of the city's town hall complex, and it would feature the return of one of her much-loved student proteges Jonathan Elsom to play the Chorus. It would be the last of her eighteen productions of Shakespeare plays, and her penultimate production ever.

It takes an act of imagination to connect both theatrical events, but it is worth the effort, for it adds to our understanding both of Ngaio Marsh the author of detective fiction and of the society of which she came to be so prominent a national figure. Marsh's passion for theatre was unbounded, and it's in her involvement with the stage that we see the greatest evidence of a passionate life, lived to the full.

43

In between the two theatrical openings lies the story of a life filled with theatre, a life in which Marsh balanced the solitary, private act of crime authorship with a very public involvement with others. The shy and somewhat reclusive writer was transformed into the confident, inspiring authority who influenced two generations of theatre-goers in their perceptions of Shakespeare. It was as much for her dramatic work as her authorship that she would enjoy a national reputation in New Zealand, that her patronage was sought, and that her opinions on a diverse range of topics were listened to.   And it was for her contribution to theatre, not literature, that she would receive an Honorary Doctorate from the University of Canterbury, and be created DBE (Dame Commander of the British Empire, the female equivalent of a knighthood).

Her family background had a profound influence on her theatrical inclinations.   Her grandfather was Edward Seager, a farsighted and in many ways liberal superintendent of the Christchurch mental asylum, where he organized theatrical entertainments for the inmates and had a small hall-cum-theatre built on the site. Marsh's mother Rose was an accomplished amateur actress, the quality of whose performances was good enough for her to consider, but eventually reject, several invitations to perform professionally.

Marsh's childhood was scented with the smell of greasepaint, for her parents met while involved with amateur theatricals, and her mother continued to act when she was growing up. Although rehearsals were unsettling to the little girl, who felt that during them her mother became a stranger, she loved hearing theatre-talk. Later, Marsh would recall: "When I was big enough to be taken occasionally to the play my joy was almost unendurable" (1). And aged twelve, she wrote in her journal, "We went to the play called Bluebell today so you may guess how excited we were before we started. It was glorious I never enjoyed myself so much in my life" (2).

Many years later, when describing the theatre-going community in New Zealand, Marsh would think nostalgically of those early days:

> There are now elderly theatre-goers whose
> memory reaches back to the times when
> there were many touring companies in our
> country, the times when gallery queues
> began to form in the early afternoon, when
> world-celebrated players came before us,
> when dramatic criticism was stringent and
> informed and eagerly read; the times when,
> in spite of greater delays in travelling, our
> theatrical link with the European roots of
> our civilisation was much stronger and more
> vigorous than it is today. These elderly
> theatre-goers, having the smell of grease-
> paint and glue size in their nostrils, and the
> active sense of an expectant audience in their
> bones, are theatre-minded in the sense that
> modern audiences in London or New York
> or Paris....are theatre-minded (3).

She was interested in drama at school, and was introduced to the study of Shakespeare by some inspiring teachers. Then, at the age of eighteen, she wrote and helped stage the production of *The Moon Princess* in the hall of St. Michael's Church, where she was a parishioner. Based on a fairytale, it has a rather fancifully versified and stilted text, but the layout of the promptbook shows a pattern of theatrical preparation which would be typical of Marsh for the rest of her life. Although the action, in which Ngaio assisted the direction of her friend Helen Burton, sometimes lapses into a contrived picturesqueness, it is still a most impressive piece of juvenilia. The script has well-spaced dances and musical interludes and a feeling for theatrical shape. The performances featured Marsh's mother, who played the witch with considerable histrionic power.

Given Marsh's well-established interest and ability in art, it's not surprising that, after secondary school, she went on to study at the Canterbury College School of Art. Theatre studies did not exist at any level of the education system, and despite the thriving professional theatre scene, with a number of touring companies presenting everything from music-hall and variety to grand opera, the theatre was still not a respectable place of work for a young woman from a middle-class family. Despite her sustained activity on the stage, the rather emotionally buttoned-up Mrs. Marsh was suspicious of the theatre. She had once told her daughter that the life of the professional actor was "too messy," and Marsh wondered if the easy emotionalism and bohemian habits of theatre people offended her natural fastidiousness (4).

All the same, the stage exerted its old fascination when during student days Marsh saw the Allan Wilkie Company in a performance of *Hamlet*:

> Since three o'clock we had waited on an iron
> staircase in a cold wind for the early doors to
> open. The play was *Hamlet*, the house was
> full and the Dane was Allan Wilkie. Thirty
> years later, when I produced the play, I
> remembered how, at the climax of the Mouse-
> trap Scene, Hamlet had stood before the King
> and had flung his script high in the air and how
> the leaves had fluttered down in a crescent as
> the curtains fell. When, so long afterwards, I

> asked my young Hamlet to repeat this business,
> the years ebbed back on a wave of nostalgia
> and gratitude and there I was, on a wooden
> bench, clapping my palms sore, on what was
> perhaps the most exciting night I was ever to
> know in the theatre (5).

In the mould of the Victorian actor-manager, and like his contemporary Donald Wolfit, Wilkie toured the British Empire with his actress wife and company of performers, presenting a wide variety of plays, but with a special focus on Shakespeare. Wilkie's influence on Marsh was powerful, for she joined his company for a short tour of New Zealand in 1919. Although none of the plays she appeared in was Shakespearean, from her mentor she gained an attitude towards direction and an understanding of how Shakespeare could be played, which shaped her subsequent career (6). Something, too, of the seriousness of his approach rubbed off; to Wilkie, Shakespeare was not only good box office, but he *mattered* in a way that no other playwright did. At his death in 1970, Marsh wrote in tribute of the actor-manager:

> Though in these antipodes he is unknown to
> our youth, we owe to him in a large measure
> what sense they may have inherited of the
> inextinguishable quality of Shakespeare as a
> workable playwright (7).

Less influential, but still instructive, were a brief involvement in the Rosemary Rees English Comedy Company and a tour of a one-act play of her own, *Little Housebound*, to two provincial towns in the North Island. For the remainder of the 1920's, Marsh's theatrical involvement was with Charities Unlimited, which mounted an annual pantomime as a fundraiser. This required her to direct large numbers of performers, experience which she would later put to great use.

In 1928, Marsh sailed for England, where she spent the next four years. Among the plays which she saw in London, she was particularly struck by Tyrone Guthrie's production of Pirandello's *Six Characters in Search of an Author*. She wrote:

> If you long above everything to be a director, this is the play that nags and clamours to be done. I was broody with it, off and on, for some eighteen years before I finally got it out of my system in a burst of three separate productions in three separate countries...It remains, to my mind, more absolutely the pure material of theatre than any other piece of twentieth-century dramatic writing. One may discount its philosophy and dismiss its meta-physics (I do not altogether do so) but tackle it simply as something that happens in a working theatre and it crackles with immediacy (8).

While in England, her writing of detective fiction began, and with it the beginning of her rise to international prominence. After a return to New Zealand in 1932 because of the declining health of her mother, who died at the end of the year, Marsh eventually resumed her directing.

The professional circuit was now dead, killed by the Depression, the popularity of the cinema, and increased costs of touring. However, the amateur theatre was in good heart, for the British Drama League, with the various regional repertory theatre societies, carried on quite vigorous production and performance of mainly contemporary British plays. Marsh's developing reputation let her adjudicate at theatre festivals and direct a number of productions in the following ten years, with a working method now firmly-established.

As her fondness for Shakespeare was not widespread, Marsh contented herself with producing works by John Drinkwater, Noel Coward, and Emlyn Williams, whose *The Corn Is Green* she directed for the Wellington Repertory Theatre in 1943. Its leading actor vividly remembers her contribution:

> Just to listen to and endeavour to emulate
> Ngaio Marsh's superb production of her own
> voice went a long way towards our learning
> to speak out so that we would be heard even
> in a low pitch in the back row, a facility per-
> haps not so necessary now in these days of
> intimate theatre. She would orchestrate our
> productions so that we were always building
> up to an important point and then relaxing,
> or, as she would say, "end of tension" (9).

Part of the sense of authority which was, it seems, perceived by everyone who came into contact with Marsh, came from her meticulous preparation. Happily, for the theatre historian, she wrote everything down in voluminous promptbooks, which today serve as the basis of the study of her plays. Even better, not only did she write in minute detail a record of the actor movement and reaction, but she sketched them. The promptbooks contain many of her drawings, usually done in pencil, illustrating the climactic moment on a particular page or a complex sequence of action. These would appear on the left-hand page of the book, the right being taken up by a cut-up or typed copy of the text, annotated with further written directions, set designs, and costume sketches.

Some of these designs are in watercolor, and they reveal a confident visual sense with considerable pictorial expressiveness. The sketches of the 1944 production of Alexander Afinogenev's *Distant Point* are extremely detailed, the costumes revealing a careful reading of the play, but adding further characterful touches. Her set designs for the same production show a fairly conservative reliance on drops, borders, and wings, but are still quite arresting. The blend of comedy and pathos which pervades the play is powerfully realized, and the Chekhovian feeling of the text is manifested in appropriate visual style.

In *The Soul of Nicholas Snyders* there's even a charming homage to Van Gogh showing the encounter between the title character and the enigmatic Pedlar who is out to snare his soul. The Dutch setting of the play is captured by Marsh in a sketch recalling the painter's *The Potato Eaters*. Typically, Marsh notes, "when Pedlar is in chair he laughs, & that cues the light to glow." This is a much more effectively contrived appearance than the original stage directions, which specify merely that "a strange, freakish figure, oddly clad with a curious peaked cap upon his head...seems to appear out of the shadows and seats himself opposite Nicholas" (10).

Whether or not these images were achieved in the often rather technically-primitive theatres for which Marsh directed is a little harder to gauge. Some photographs of tableaux from the productions seem more amateurish than the promptbooks might suggest. On the other hand, it must be conceded that even today, theatrical effects are notoriously difficult to record on film. The greater limitations of lighting and photographic equipment of the past may mean that quite magical effects were impossible to capture for posterity.

It's possible that Marsh's prominence may have come about partly because of the war, which gave many women an entree to work which they might not otherwise have undertaken. However, her first Shakespearean production resulted from a more direct request: in 1941 she was approached by a group of Canterbury University College students having great problems getting their production of Sutton Vane's *Outward Bound* staged. Could she help? Marsh agreed, but on the proviso that if it worked, she be allowed to choose the next play she might direct for them. The Drama Society readily acquiesced. It was a low ebb, for the ranks of student members had been much reduced by the war, and Marsh had a very solid reputation as a professional director.

All the same, the society had a major asset in its possession, a Little Theatre which provided the frame for Marsh's early directorial triumphs. Occupying a former lecture-room on the University College site, it had real limitations, and one student performer had little love for it, considering it "to have been without doubt the nastiest stage on which I have ever had to act...; it was a box stage with almost no wings and with entry to them consisting of one 5 foot door each side. Ventilation was Nil" (11). On the other hand, another former student actor, John Pocock, describes the space in rather more glowing terms, recalling its intimacy and workshop feeling, and analyzing its effect on the style of Marsh productions:

> Most "intimate," "little" theatres produce an
> "intimate" style, set in living-rooms and tending
> to social realism...The reason the Little Theatre
> and its style (her creation) went in quite a differ-
> ent way was quite simple, I think. There was a
> cyclorama,...a permanent, shallowly curving wall
> covered with flat plaster, which ran almost from
> wall to wall of the stage area...The point about

> this cyclorama was that it could take light and
> reflect it neutrally, giving the impression of
> indefinitely deep space; and there was just
> enough lighting equipment, and just enough
> space and height above the acting area, to
> permit us to do things with this effect....This
> is important because all Ngaio's Shakespear-
> ean direction was built on the *speaking of*
> *verse* by actors *moving in space*; and the
> cyclorama created the effect (not the illusion)
> of space necessary to establish the relation
> between *verse* and *space* (12).

This Little Theatre provided the venue for what came to be dubbed the "Golden Age" of Drama Society life.

After the success of *Outward Bound*, Marsh finally presented her first Shakespeare production, the 1943 *Hamlet*. In wartime Christchurch, which had seen only a few Shakespearean plays during the previous decade, this performance was something of a sensation. Here, it seemed, was the authentic voice of Shakespearean drama, reaching out with an authority and passion to its audience, turning handicaps, such as the difficulty of clothing a cast under wartime restrictions, into triumphs. Performed in modern dress, with music by the young composer Douglas Lilburn, the production found ready critical favor and widespread public acclaim. There was alarm about the possibility of the Fire Board investigating the evident overcrowding of the theatre, and there were complaints from the police about queues outside the booking office. The show was sold out and subsequently revived for a season after the university examinations were over. Along with the next year's *Othello*, *Hamlet* was once more revived for a tour of New Zealand by

the impresario Dan O'Connor, who would develop a close relationship with the director in the ensuing years.
Marsh remembered that first Shakespearean production with great affection, returning to it often in public speeches and radio talks. In a 1962 lecture she said:

> I think all of us remember those productions chiefly for the audience's response to them. I remember one night, I looked through the wings of the Little Theatre and saw, standing by the stage with his forearm resting on it, so close to the actors that they might have touched him, a young New Zealander. His face was caught in the reflected light from the stage and he was perfectly still. For as long as I watched, there he was, motionless. When I asked the actors if they had noticed him, I found that none of them had done so. It was really a case of perfect relationship between the stage and the auditorium (13).

Some of the visual effects were particularly striking, and there's an assurance about grouping and actor movement which is still most impressive. With this group of students, Marsh had found her theatrical metier: an enthusiastic, intelligent band of youthful performers which was hungry for work and eager to fulfill her vision. Her work with the Drama Society would continue almost to the end of her life.

What cannot be deduced from Marsh's meticulous promptbooks is her skill at casting, especially during the early years. She was able to exploit particular strengths of individual performers to allow them to create memorable characterizations. One observer said that as a director Marsh

could make virtues of her actors' deficiencies
through judicious casting and sympathetic
direction...Jack Henderson, the 1943 Hamlet,
had rather a chip on his shoulder about his
lameness, but Marsh saw in that actor's nature
an attitude which would help him express
something of the complexity and intensity of
the character he was playing. His Hamlet was
superb (14).

There's a remarkable consistency about Marsh's
Shakespeare productions. Although she read widely and
possessed a formidable intelligence, her interpretations were
not intellectual. Knowledge of twentieth-century theories
about direction, acting, and design impinged on her writing
about the theatre, but hardly at all on her practice of directing
for the stage--unless she had a student designer or stage
manager who could suggest innovations. These would often
be taken up with alacrity. Although she believed in ensemble
acting--indeed, demanded it from her cast members--Marsh
still relied on the "star quality" of her leading performers. Yet
she could be dismissive of "operatic" productions which
featured a star actor whose performance glittered because of
the prevailing dullness of the acting surrounding him. In a
scrapbook which Marsh kept of her theatre-going in London
during the late 1940's, the programs for Donald Wolfit's
performances received some particularly sharp annotations.

To Marsh, the text of a Shakespeare play was of
primary importance, and at its core was a single idea, which
the director had to discover and then manifest onstage. She
would argue this case with some eloquence, saying:

The first duty of the producer is to make up
his mind if possible in Stanislavsky's one word

what the play is about. Sometimes it jumps
to the eye. *Macbeth*, he may decide, is about
ambition, *Othello* about jealousy, *Hamlet*
about death. But what is *Lear* about, what
The Tempest? Within the confines of his
own understanding, the producer must
know. However complex the writing, however rich the texture, however distracting
the subplots, at the core of Shakespeare's
major works, there is a single dominant idea.
Let him disbelieve this, and the producer
becomes a prey to notions, trimmings, and
every kind of impertinence. It's when he's
most vividly certain of the core of the play
that he comes closest to his author (15).

In *A Play Toward*, a book which describes her
approach to play direction, Marsh advised would-be directors
to orchestrate the play in their minds and fit the actors into the
model which the promptbook provided. But, if this were done
long before the first rehearsal, and before even the casting
auditions, to what extent were the actors behaving as anything
other than directorial puppets? Marsh was uncompromising
about this point:

The actor-director relationship is always a
complex one. In Shakespeare it is particularly so. The plays are wide open to every
kind of treatment. If the director fails to
convince his actors that his reading is a valid
one, he is in for trouble. Actors are not
naturally inclined to think of themselves as
integrated parts of a conception, but rather
as a collection of soloists. It is their produ-

cer's job to reconcile them to a scheme of
orchestration. If he succeeds in doing this,
they give him everything (16).

A powerful orchestrator, Marsh was always in
interpretative charge, and there was little warbling of native
wood-notes wild during the playing of her score. In *Passing
Through* (17), a recent one-man play which touches on
Mervyn Thompson's experience as a student actor in her
productions, there's a revealing section in which he re-enacts
Marsh directing a young actor, explaining a complete
character profile as a way of tackling a tricky speech. Every
detail of the director's analysis is convincing, and all the focus
is on helping the performer understand the psychological
make-up of his role as a way of making sense of his words.
The insights are deep, but they remain ineluctably those of the
director, and not the actor. The process is that of instruction,
not joint discovery.
Writing of the 1964 *Julius Caesar*, the same
playwright remembered enjoying it

mainly for its thrilling crowd scenes and for
Barry Empson (Casca) and David Hindin
(Brutus). David was one of the few actors
who was able, within the regimentation of
Ngaio's work, to move an audience with his
total humanity. With many performers,
Ngaio's direction, while always powerful,
appeared "glued on" (18).

He added, "I don't think actors *dared* make too many
suggestions--but in any case Ngaio knew the plays backwards
and was normally way ahead of her actors."

The directorial grasp of the play was indeed considerable, and the audition notices for her productions contain succinct character summaries which reveal how much Marsh had crystallized her thoughts about the roles which actors were seeking. The notice for the last Shakespearean production, *Henry V* in 1972, is typically forthright in its demands of the male characters. Marsh describes Henry as:

> not a two-dimensional chauvinistic princeling
> but a lonely young man at the top, carrying a
> load of inherited guilt and a heavy responsibility.
> There are echoes of the irresponsibly practical
> joker of Henry IV. Altogether he is a much
> more complex and subtle character than he is
> commonly supposed to be. He is in turn deeply
> religious, gay, oppressed, compassionate, ruth-
> less. He knows and is appalled by the horrors
> of warfare and yet is a brilliant soldier.
>
> Wanted: A good voice and carriage. A warm
> personality and that indefinable asset: "star
> quality." Also a player who can see beyond
> the popular facade of the King and give us the
> full man.

The female characters are sketched in more briefly, however. According to Marsh, Mistress Quickly has:

> in the past, "obliged" Falstaff in every sense
> of the Phrase and is a bawdy lady turned
> groggily respectable. Shakespeare has
> rewarded her with one of the most rivetting
> descriptions of a death, in the whole range
> of dramatic literature.

Wanted: An Actress (19)

The brevity of the final casting demand points up
another interesting feature of Marsh's career as a director--the
closeness of her relationship with her leading actors.
Actresses fared less well, on the whole. Marsh was unfailingly
polite to all, but she was closer to her male proteges than her
female ones.   Of course, there's the obvious fact that
Shakespearean plays favor male performers in terms of range
of characters, but in private, Marsh made clear her feelings
about the quality of the women who auditioned for some
productions. In letters she wrote to a friend in 1963 during
rehearsals for *Henry IV Part One* she considered it

> an odd circumstance that [female] under-
> graduates with talent are always hard to find.
> Few come up for auditions & of those few
> only a handful, over the years, have approach-
> ed the level of the men...*Why*, I wonder, out
> of some 2000 undergraduates is there never a
> better haul? Are they too anxiously involved
> in adolescent sex? Or what? (20)

Nevertheless, Marsh engendered a fierce loyalty and
commitment among the student actors who liked her
approach. Casting was very competitive, and the director had
a wide range of aspirants to choose from.   She was
adventurous in giving major parts to new talent, but the
secondary roles were often filled by older performers who
returned to the Drama Society long after they had left
university. Sometimes, proteges such as Jonathan Elsom and
Elric Hooper would be invited back from their well-
established overseas careers to star, while others, like Gerald
Lascelles, who had continued to live in Christchurch, would

help to organize the productions and play supporting roles. Their performances gave lustre and solidity to the productions and helped reinforce the "house style" of the Shakespearean plays. Mervyn Thompson considered that Marsh was a puppeteer, but added "some of the puppets became Pinnochios" (21). However, his view would not be shared by those whose association with Marsh lasted a number of years. In 1972, Gerald Lascelles wrote warmly of his mentor's approach to directing Shakespeare:

> At a somewhat superficial level, the first thing one notices is the speed with which she works. I remember my first rehearsal with her some years ago when, in one evening's work, she blocked out three or four major Shakespearean scenes; a feat accomplished only by careful and intensive preparation....Some directors may contend that such organization leads to a certain inflexibility but when one is shaping inexperience, working with the most complex of plays and running against the clock, there is no question which is the right approach. Nor will one ever find her casts accusing her of inflexibility. Few directors can be more responsive to new suggestions and to different approaches to a dramatic problem and if someone else's ideas "work," and are consistent with the overall conception, in they may go (22).

How should an actor develop a Shakespearean role? Despite suggesting that an actor should "find parallels in his experience for the emotions he must interpret" (23), Marsh considered the Method approach unsuited to the plays of

Shakespeare, declaring that "it can be, and often is, wildly irrelevant. It can have as little effect upon the dynamic of the play as petit point embroidery upon a backdrop" (24).

Marsh's direction was architectural, in the sense that every element was designed to fit in with the overall plan, but it was also organic. Marsh's assurance in creating pattern in time and space can be seen not only in the fluent illustrations adorning the promptbooks, but the way in which photographs show her positioning actors with vigor and feel for contrast. The plasticity of movement in her direction and the manipulation of spacing, height, and grouping to intensify climaxes show that a master of visual rhetoric is at work. Mervyn Thompson defined the essence of her directorial style in the following crisp phrases:

> Everything in large sweeps. Spectacular vis-
> ual patterns. Emphasis on swift movement
> forward of narrative. Rousing climaxes!
> Large emphasis on tonal variations. Character
> secondary to "musical" elements. Good
> "popular" Shakespeare. Great "orchestration."
> Nothing "dry" left in. Not much in the way of
> politics either (25).

Having marked the rhetorical and emotional peaks and foothills into her script, Marsh was able to work them up into theatrically-satisfying action. The big scenes were, according to one observer, "sharply realized and visually exaggerated," (26) and nowhere is this more evident than in her productions of *Julius Caesar*.

For many of the participants in the 1953 *Caesar*, the experience of rehearsal was fascinating. Mrs. Ann Shearer remembers that it

was hugely exciting to watch N. M. at work.
Her ability to concentrate on a tiny detail,
while keeping the shape of the whole in her
mind, was fascinating.   N. M. usually wore
black trousers, a jersey, a silky scarf or
flamboyant pendant, and a jacket over her
shoulders. She smoked endlessly. Her handsome appearance, which changed little in later
years, and her beautiful distinctive deep voice
made her a compelling personality. She had
a minutely annotated text and she talked frequently to other shadowy, authoritative figures
who I now realize must have been the production secretary, stage manager and so on...

N. M.'s stillness and concentration won from
the whole cast a devoted respect and desire
to realise her vision. She was fairly austere,
although undoubtedly the older and more
mature actors had some sort of intimacy with
her. She had a formidable quality which
discouraged any slackness or nonsense among
the cast, yet she could be very patient and gentle with an actor who couldn't manage what she
wanted. She spoke the lines superbly herself,
with great variation of pace and pitch. She also
moved about the acting area with freedom and
style, demonstrating what she wanted.

She was very meticulous about certain stresses
and intonations. One line sticks in my mind:
"It is the bright day that brings forth the adder,
and that craves wary walking." The lack of

obvious iambic stresses in the first part leads
and inexperienced verse speaker to seek them
in the second: "and thát craves wáry wálking."
But N. M. wanted "and that cráves wáry
wálking"--ie, Brutus is till referring to the dan-
gers of the bright day in general, & not specifically the peril of the snake. She also wanted
a glottal stop at the beginning of "adder," to
avoid the ugly y-liaison "thee yadder" (27).

Marsh's command of her scripts was not only
interpretive, but based on memory. She habitually had a
word-perfect knowledge of the entire play under rehearsal,
and to her the speaking of words was very important. Indeed,
she maintained that the solution to textual problems could
often be found not in literary study of the plays, but through
saying the words aloud. In a lecture, she declared that she
had

found so often that the pundits who have no
knowledge whatever of the theatre as a
working-house--quick forge and working-
house of thought--they make a terrific mouth-
ful of something that when an actor gets here
and says it, becomes perfectly clear, because
in Shakespeare, sound and sense are one. And
he wrote with the best sounds to project what
he wanted to give. Sound and sense are one,
and when you're muddling away about what
precisely does that phrase mean, if you stand
up and say it, listening to the sound of it, you'll
find the door to interpretation has opened
when you weren't looking (28).

Marsh recommended the use of the British publication *A Manual of Practice in Speechcraft* (29), and her own habit of teaching her New Zealand actors remained unchanged through the years. They were trained to abandon their own accent, which she considered "an unsatisfactory vehicle for the magnificent words" of Shakespeare (30). In her view--one entirely consistent with her upbringing, early theatrical experience, social class, and the then-current attitude that Great Britain was the source of all culture--actors *had* to adopt the dialect of the upper-middle classes living in the southeast of England. That this was as foreign to the speech of Shakespeare as the despised New Zealand dialect was an inconsistency which she only rarely alluded to, and never resolved.

There was, similarly, no differentiation in the Marsh approach between the demanding task of giving her inexperienced young actors some vocal technique--teaching them how to breathe, articulate consonants, project and color their speech, and make sense of the complex rhythms of blank verse--and getting them to use a particular accent. That's not to deny, of course, that when cast members could rise to the challenge of adopting the vocal idiom which Marsh sought, the results could be compelling and effective.

This was perhaps most noticeable in the "big production numbers". from the plays: scenes involving rhetorical intensity or oratory. Above all else, Marsh wanted to make her beloved Shakespeare's text live on the stage. When Mark Antony faced the crowd in her productions of *Julius Caesar*, they yelled "Brutus" at him. Marsh asked a student audience:

What does he say? He says something that
all of you have said over and over again.

"Friends, Romans, countrymen, lend me
your *ears*." And practically every actor that
plays the part says it with that stress. But
isn't he perhaps saying, "Friends!" Roars and
yells from the Romans. "Romans!" More
jeers and yells. "Countrymen!" More jeers
and yells. "Lend *me* your ears. (Not Brutus)"
(31).

Was part of Marsh's success at working with largely
untrained actors due to the fact that they were untrained? It's
a tantalizing question, for it's surely significant that in her one
major attempt at establishing and directing a professional
company, Marsh was less successful than she had been before
then, or would be in subsequent years.

The British Commonwealth Theatre Company began
with high hopes and extensive auditions in the United
Kingdom. Interviewed in 1951 about the group, Marsh said,
"it's designed to [bind] the players, for the most part young
professional actors and actresses from Great Britain and all the
countries of the Commonwealth, into a unit and to play
throughout their own countries and in Great Britain" (32).
Under-capitalized, based on a model which suited the 1920's
in terms of costs, the venture came to a premature close.
Early in the tour of Australia, there was dissension among the
cast, and box-office receipts failed to cover costs. As the tour
continued into New Zealand, audiences recovered somewhat,
but Marsh's failing health, and the worsening balance sheet,
contributed to the company's demise after its six-month period
of confirmed theatre bookings had elapsed.

The omens for a fully-professional set-up had been
more positive than this rather ignominious result might
suggest. The Old Vic company had completed a highly
successful tour of Australia and New Zealand in 1948, but

then it had had the glamour of Laurence Olivier and Vivien
Leigh to boost the box office. Marsh's student player tours of
New Zealand in 1944, and Australia in 1949, had received
widespread publicity and drawn sizeable, keen audiences.
There was a tight sense of ensemble about the group of unpaid
performers and backstage workers, but creating and sustaining
a successful professional company proved to be rather a
different proposition.

In a radio talk Marsh glossed over the internal ructions
and unhappiness of the group, and instead talked with some--
evidently justified--asperity of the decrepit conditions of the
theatres in which they performed. In one theatre, she said,

> rain poured in through the roof into the filthy
> dressing-rooms and drifted across the rat-
> eaten stage. It's out of the question to expect
> a professional actor or theatre producer to
> work under such conditions. My own com-
> pany behaved admirably, but they couldn't,
> even if it were possible to do so, repeat such
> experience (33).

One of her student actors in the 1940's considers that Marsh
"was sometimes over-respectful of professionals, and they--
being what they are--didn't always respect her in return...She
was better at writing about professional actors than at working
with them" (34).

In the promptbooks for the British Commonwealth
Theatre Company productions, there is a revealing
manifestation of Marsh's working methods, one which
indicates that her approach to contemporary plays was the
same as for Shakespeare, and that working with professionals
was the same as working with students. The opening of *Six
Characters in Search of an Author* reveals the orchestrator at

work, expanding and elaborating the rather brief printed stage
directions, which say:

> The spectators will find the curtain raised and
> the stage as it usually is during the day time....
> so that from the beginning the public may have
> the impression of an impromptu performance.

> The actors and actresses of the company enter
> from the back of the stage: first one, then an-
> other, then two together; nine or ten in all.
> They are about to rehearse a Pirandello play:
> "Mixing it Up." Some of the company move
> off toward their dressing rooms. The prompter
> who has the "book" under his arm is waiting
> for the manager in order to begin the rehearsal.
> The actors and actresses, some standing, some
> sitting, chat and smoke. One perhaps reads a
> paper, another cons his part.

Under Marsh's direction, early rehearsals would
involve blocking the following detailed instructions:

> Orchestra comes in. Max focusing lights and
> talking to band. Stage hand enter from audi-
> ence. 5 Chairs piles up on stage. Stage hand
> bring four down to table and arrange as above.
> Whistling. Sit on table. Light cigarette.

> Character Woman on from house. Sit on box.
> Goloshes. "Good morning." Stage hand:
> "Morning lady. Nice morning." "Lovely"
> Character Woman take out knitting. Stage
> hand up to back of set Right. Read magazine.

Ngaio as a young performer, courtesy of Aitken, Stone & Wylie, London, agents for the Ngaio Marsh estate.

Top left: Ngaio in the spotlight, courtesy of the Macmillan Brown Library, University of Canterbury, New Zealand.
Top right: Ngaio in mid-career, courtesy of the Harvard Theatre Library Collection, Harvard University, Cambridge, Massachusetts.
Bottom: Ngaio at work on a detective novel in her London flat.

Top: Marc Anthony confronts the Roman crowd, 1953 production of Julius Caesar.

Bottom left: Promptbook sketch of the death of Cinna, the poet; 1964 production of Julius Caesar. University of Canterbury Drama Society, Courtesy of the Macmillan Brown Library, University of Canterbury, New Zealand.

Bottom right: Ngaio after receiving an honorary doctorate in literature from the University of Canterbury (1962). Courtesy of Aitken, Stone & Wylie, agents for the Ngaio Marsh estate.

Top left: Ngaio gardens on the balcony of her London flat, courtesy of Aitken, Stone & Wylie.

Top right: Ngaio at the wheel of her Jaguar XK150. Photograph by David Palmer, courtesy of Dr. Margaret Lewis.

Bottom left: Ngaio, at work on a novel. Photograph by J. Claude-Benson, courtesy of Dr. Margaret Lewis.

Bottom right: Ngaio holding her Edgar Award upon being made a Grand Master (1978). Photograph by Suzanne Richards, courtesy of Bruce Harding.

Left: Page from Ngaio's promptbook showing blocking for Macbeth.
Right: Ngaio's sketch for banqueting scene from Macbeth. Both photographs courtesy of the Alexander Turnbull Library, Wellington, New Zealand.

Exit whistling up Right.

Wardrobe Woman enter from house. Up to Character Woman. "Good Morning, Miss Delaney." "Good morning, dear." "Wardrobe Woman looks at knitting. Business & gagging. Wardrobe woman exits left, comes out sewing and sits down in auditorium, working. Orchestra tune up. Music.

Second Juvenile to Wardrobe Woman.

Ingenue from house. Squat by Character Woman. They measure knitting and gag.

Juvenile from house, singing. Very gay. "Good morning, good morning, you're looking very beautiful, Mrs Delaney." Business with scarf & gag & mug. Then Juvenile to stage hand up Right. Juvenile cons part.

Leading Man from house with newspaper. "Good Morning, ladies." Lounge on bench left. Read newspaper. Turn away. Take out part. "God what a life." (Light cigarette)

Leading Lady from house. Leading Man up. Elaborate greetings. Left Centre. Juvenile offer cigarette. Leading Man light it. Stage hand bring chair and cross downstage to Juvenile. (35)

Such a degree of predefined action may have been unpopular with a professional cast, but it paid off handsomely in the production which would mark Marsh's return to Shakespeare with the Drama Society. In some ways, it was like the *Hamlet* of ten years before, for it signalled Marsh's reassertion of her powers as a director after the collapse of the professional company, and it also represented a new start for the Drama Society. In 1952 the group had lost its home when the Little Theatre had been destroyed by fire, so the mounting of so large-scale a production as *Julius Caesar* the following year was a way of declaring confidence in its future.

Because of the loss of the theatre, an amphitheatre was specially built in the Great Hall of the University College, making this production the first arena production of Shakespeare in New Zealand. This break with theatrical orthodoxy was the subject of much comment, for it provided a shallow acting-space surrounded on three sides by banks of steeply-raked seating. The set design by the sculptor Tom Taylor, then a fine arts student, contained a spiral staircase curving round a central rotating tower. This was positioned on top of three sharply-ascending flights of steps, and reached by tunnels which went underneath the seating. The primary benefit was to give extra power, focus, and fluency to the crowd scenes with which Marsh filled the play.

The crowd was the dominant character in this production. It seemed to one critic "as tumultuous and vociferous as the most insurrectionary demagogue would like" (36), and many were impressed by an intensity which proximity lent to the action. The promptbook reveals a mastery of gesture, movement pattern, and focal emphasis, especially in the positioning of principal characters who were treated rather like soloists in a symphonic score. Marsh's directions run as a kind of subtext under the lines, commenting, expanding, underscoring the action's "big moments" with considerable gusto.

The result is a racy, exciting version of the play, one which, without eschewing the tenderness of more intimate scenes like that between Brutus and Portia, places its emphasis firmly on the public side of the text. Despite her professed desire to have the director represent the essence of the play, Marsh cut and amended the text of all of her plays. *Julius Caesar*, for example, has 138 such changes, including the deletion of nearly all the supernatural influences, the abbreviation of the last two acts' political intrigue, and the representation of battle by symbolic action involving the swirling-about of sets of flags.

The later 1964 version of the play, which Marsh intended to be her final production for the Drama Society, would involve the use of a script for improvisation by the crowd. In fact, it is a very tightly-constructed piece of writing, containing lines from *Coriolanus* and the history plays, as well as phrases of directorial invention, such as, "Ensanguined butchers. Tell us, if you can, why you so acted!" (37) Individual crowd members speak lines which articulate the shifting emotions of the sub-group they represent, and the script lays bare the organization and overlapping of their cries, gasps, and expressions of mounting anger. Marsh said of *Julius Caesar* that

> the play might be subtitled "The Mob." To
> a very great extent, it depends on a concerted,
> eloquent and organised crowd, so articulated
> that each individual is given an opportunity to
> develop and project a clearly defined person-
> ality (38).

This stress on the crowd clearly worked, but whether or not it accurately reflects the play is a moot point. It's an exaggeration for Marsh to assert that the mob really dominates three-quarters of the play. In fact, in the original text it appears in only a few scenes, and not at all during the assassination or the final two acts. Marsh's crowd was present during the whole of the assassination, thus accentuating the power of Mark Anthony's speeches, which were considered a thoroughgoing piece of demagoguery.

The postwar years saw a solid cluster of productions up to 1964, on a semi-annual basis, and fitted around Marsh's writing and frequent visits to London. The Shakespeare performances which followed after were "special" productions of one sort or another. The 1967 *Twelfth Night* marked the opening of the theatre which the University of Canterbury named in her honor; the 1969 *Midsummer Night's Dream* featured the return of Elric Hooper (who had played Hamlet in 1958) from the London stage, and also the performance of Sam Neill in a minor role; the production of *King Henry V* in 1972 had a celebratory and civic function. Marsh's last production was of *Sweet Mr Shakespeare*, a solo show featuring another returned student actor, Jonathan Elsom, playing Shakespeare and performing a sequence drawn from the Sonnets.

Long before her death, Marsh was a major figure in the cultural landscape in New Zealand. She delivered the prestigious MacMillan Brown Lectures in 1962, collectively entitled *The Three Cornered World*, which dealt with the nature of theatre. She wrote, lectured, and broadcast with vigor, and remained secure in her position as a figure of the establishment in Christchurch, surrounded by a small circle of close friends.

What, then, did she achieve through all those years of dramatic activity?

In her autobiography Marsh writes movingly of the transient nature of the passion which was, one could argue, closer to her heart than that of detective fiction:

> Theatrical endeavour is the most ephemeral of all the arts. When a season comes to an end, it does so abruptly and completely and if, in whatever form and however explicitly or abstractly the cloud-capped towers and gorgeous palaces may have been suggested, they do indeed melt into air, into thin air. Canvas flats, stacked against a wall, a bare stage, a folded cyclorama and dust are all that is left of Illyria or the road to Dover, of Agincourt or Elsinore or the Blasted Heath (39).

The cadence of regret in those words is unmistakable, and they succinctly summarize the predicament facing the theatre historian, who must try to imaginatively recreate the performances which once existed onstage, using the available sources of information. Always, however, the doubt remains, and one wonders: "Was it really like this?" The process is much less direct than, say, that of studying the detective fiction, for there one can simply open a book and be in immediate contact with the writer.

As the unforgiving years pass, the numbers of those who saw or took part in the Marsh productions diminish, the collective memory of her achievement fades, and the assessment of her place in theatrical history becomes more difficult. Nevertheless, by any standards--length of career, quality of productions, impact on the theatre scene--her reputation must be secure within New Zealand. No other director here has had so sustained a career, and of the quality of the best of her Shakespearean productions there can be no doubt.

And yet, she belongs irretrievably to the past. There is no school of Marsh actors or directors; her method of directing can be described as belonging to the style of the actor-manager; her productions can be fairly judged both apolitical and Anglocentric. To assess her place in history, we need that sense of perspective which time lends, even to the transient happenings on the stage. We cannot wholly reclaim the past, but then neither should we forget it.

What can't be denied, and what should be celebrated, is the encouragement which many theatre professionals first received at her hands. It's certain that without Ngaio Marsh's contribution to drama in New Zealand, a diverse range of theatre people would have had a less memorable, less vital introduction to a passion for theatre. Moreover, the Marsh productions gave pleasure to audiences literally for generations. It's a splendid legacy.

ENDNOTES

1. Ngaio Marsh, *Black Beech and Honeydew,* Rev. ed. (Auckland: Fontana/Collins, 1984), 28; hereafter cited as *BBHD*.
2. Margaret Lewis, *Ngaio Marsh: A Life* (Wellington: Bridget Williams Books, 1991), 12.
3. Ngaio Marsh, "Marsh speaks on drama in NZ," Radio New Zealand Sound Archive, 1952.
4. Marsh, *BBHD*, 28.
5. Marsh, *BBHD*, 120.
6. They were *The Luck of the Navy, Hindle Wakes, The Rotters,* and *A Temporary Gentleman.*

7. Ngaio Marsh, "Allan Wilkie--A Tribute," *The Press*, [Christchurch] 20 January 1970, 6.
8. Marsh, *BBHD*, 197.
9. Letter from George Vincent to Paul R. Bushnell, 8 May 1984.
10. Ngaio Marsh, *The Soul of Nicholas Snyders* promptbook, MS 1397 Folder 38 fMS 170, Alexander Turnbull Library.
11. Letter from Guy Hawley to Paul R. Bushnell, 24 July 1984.
12. Letter from J. G. A. Pocock to Paul R. Bushnell, 17 February 1984.
13. Ngaio Marsh, "The Audience," *The Three-Cornered World*, Radio New Zealand Sound Archive, 1962.
14. Personal interview with Laurence Baigent, 3 February 1984.
15. Ngaio Marsh, "The Producer," *The Three-Cornered World*, Radio New Zealand Sound Archive, 1962.
16. Marsh, "The Producer," *The Three-Cornered World*, 1962.
17. Mervyn Thompson, *Passing Through and Other Plays* (Wellington: Hazard Press, 1992).
18. Letter from Mervyn Thompson to Paul Bushnell, 11 November 1983.
19. Ngaio Marsh, "Shakespeare from a producer's viewpoint," *The Press* [Christchurch], 7 June 1962, 11.
20. Letters from Ngaio Marsh to Doris McIntosh, 9 May 1963 and 25 June 1963, in Doris, Lady McIntosh Inward Correspondence 1946-02 and 1946-03, Alexander Turnbull Library.
21. Thompson to Bushnell, 11 November 1983.
22. Gerald Lascelles, "Dame Ngaio Marsh: Director," *The Press* [Christchurch], 23 September 1972, 2.

23. Ngaio Marsh, *A Play Toward* (Christchurch: Caxton Press, 1946), 27.
24. Ngaio Marsh, "The Quick Forge," *Landfall,* 18:1 (March 1964), 37.
25. Thompson to Bushnell, 11 November 1983.
26. Baigent to Bushnell, 3 February 1984.
27. Elsie Fogerty, *A Manual of Practice in Speechcraft* (London: Dent, 1930).
28. Letter from Mrs. Ann Shearer to Paul R. Bushnell, 27 April 1984.
29. Ngaio Marsh, "Directing Shakespeare," Lecture delivered at Victoria University, Wellington, Radio New Zealand Sound Archive, 1970.
30. Ngaio Marsh, "It's Not What We Say," *New Zealand Listener,* 14 October 1978.
31. Marsh, "Directing Shakespeare."
32. Ngaio Marsh, "Ngaio Marsh speaks about the Commonwealth Players," Radio New Zealand Sound Archive, 1951.
33. Ngaio Marsh, "Marsh speaks on drama NZ," Radio New Zealand Sound Archive, 1952.
34. Pocock to Bushnell, 17 February 1984.
35. Ngaio Marsh, *Six Characters in Search of an Author* promptbook, fMS 169, Alexander Turnbull Library.
36. P. J. O. F., "As We Like It," *Canta,* 13 August 1953.
37. Archive Book, University of Canterbury Drama Society, University of Canterbury Library.
38. Ngaio Marsh, Notes, MS 1397, Alexander Turnbull Library.
39. Marsh, *BBHD,* 273.

Criminal Performances: The Spectacle of Crime in Ngaio Marsh's Detective Fiction

by Marilyn Rye

Ngaio Marsh observed about her career as a mystery writer, "...I just slid into detective writing." She had trained as a painter and worked as a director of amateur theatricals while in New Zealand. Although she had some success as a journalist and was a competent writer, her career as a detective novelist was unplanned and unexpected. Indeed, Marsh had abandoned an earlier attempt to write fiction when she put aside a serious novel about New Zealand. Like many others before her, she claimed to have written her first detective novel out of curiosity to see if she could construct a work similar to the detective novels popular with the reading public. The success of her first novel with its introduction of a new detective, Roderick Alleyn, started her down a path in a new direction, but a path that had been well traveled. While Marsh followed the classic formula of Golden Age detective fiction, she reinvigorated it by restating the familiar in unfamiliar terms. Her background in the theatre, her knowledge of art, her personal observation of the British upper classes, and her New Zealand birth allowed her to create unfamiliar but interesting settings for her crimes, develop intriguing and unusual characters, and base the solution of mysteries on the specialized knowledge of an

75

insider. Thus in her career as a writer, Marsh drew upon expertise and interests from several areas of her life. When reading a Marsh novel, readers immediately realize that theatre was one of Marsh's most passionate interests. Similarly, critics have recognized the influence of Marsh's theatrical experience on her work. Several critics have looked at Marsh's explicit use of theatrical settings in novels such as *Enter a Murderer* or her last novel, *Light Thickens*.

For example, the critic Earl F. Bargainnier has made an extensive inventory of the direct theatrical references in Marsh's work, examining all of her novels with theatrical settings or characters and tracing the impact of Roderick Alleyn's theatrical knowledge. Obviously, Marsh's novels using theatrical settings call on her knowledge of an actor's psychology and the mechanics of performance to plot the crime, develop the mystery, and create authentic backgrounds. The influence of her theatrical background on her other novels is also important and deserves the same kind of attention. Many of her novels which do not deal directly with theatrical experiences still emphasize the theatrical elements of a case. The Lamprey children's charade in *Death of a Peer* is a good example of a performance outside of the theatre that sets the stage for murder. When in *The Nursing Home Murder* Alleyn realizes the parallels between the operating theatre and a public theatre, he begins to suspect that a murderer has played the role of innocent bystander. A title like *Enter a Murderer* also suggests the parallel Marsh saw between criminal performances and acting. So does her use of theatrical performances in nontheatrical settings in many of her other novels. Examples such as these suggest the value of examining the ways Marsh extends her theatrical vision to nontheatrical settings where criminals, like actors, create false appearances and play roles that conceal their true identities as murderers. In particular, Marsh reinforces the identification of murdering and acting through the use of her detective, Roderick Alleyn, who functions as both an audience to criminal performances and a performer/director in his own right.

Margaret Lewis, in her recent biography of Marsh, assigns Marsh's fiction to the second Golden Age of detective fiction as defined by Julian Symons (1). Although Marsh's work extends beyond Symons's terminal date of World War II for the second stage, her works continued to use the conventions developed during the prewar period of the "whodunit." In his essay, "The Typology of Detective Fiction," Todorov demonstrates that the identifying characteristic of the whodunit lies in its structure of a double narrative, "the story of the crime and the story of the investigation...[which] in their purest form have no point in common" (2). The whodunit suppresses the first narrative and focuses on the second narrative which Todorov deems "excessive" and sees as only serving the purpose of conveying the first narrative to the reader. Although I disagree with his evaluation of the investigatory narrative as "insignificant," his characterization of the first narrative as an absent narrative "...which cannot be immediately present in the book" (3) explains the important role sustaining illusion plays in the whodunit. Todorov's discussion of absence highlights the way the criminal characters present themselves in an illusory way to the other characters. Their real actions and history are part of the absent narrative which they work to keep absent or hidden. The second narrative of the whodunit centers around the conflict between the criminal who wants to sustain illusions and the detective who needs to recognize and strip them away. Looked at in this light, the covering up of crime becomes a performance with the criminal's objective mimicking that of the theatrical performer: sustaining illusions that audiences are persuaded to accept as real. The detective is the critical audience who recognizes that the performance is a production.

Because her theatrical background makes her highly aware of the role of unmasking illusion in a fictional criminal investigation, Marsh frequently sets her stories either within a theatre or creates a mystery that unfolds in connection with a deliberately devised performance or a fortuitous one. Like the two characters who die in the middle of stage dramas, Surbonadier as the Beaver in *Enter a Murderer* and Dougal Macdougal as Macbeth in *Light Thickens*, Carlos Rivera in *A Wreath for Rivera* dies while playing the accordion in a nightclub performance and old William Andersen dies in the role of the Fool at the Mardian sword dance in *Death of a Fool*. Present by coincidence, Alleyn sees the murders of Surbonadier, Macdougal, and Rivera take place, whereas he reconstructs the performance of the sword dance. In *Spinsters in Jeopardy*, Alleyn, as well as his wife, Troy, sees the murder of Grizel Locke at the Château de la Chèvre d'Argent in what appears as an illuminated tableau framed by the castle's window. Marsh weaves an amateur theatrical into the plot of *Death of a Peer* and a Maori entertainment into *Colour Scheme*. Marsh's conscious use of theatrical metaphors to describe other events heightens the reader's awareness of their contrived nature and the duplicitous purpose behind their arrangement.

The apparent murder attempt on the President of Ng'ombwana, affectionately called "the Boomer" by his former schoolmate Alleyn, exemplifies the way Marsh draws attention to the illusion of appearances. The plot of *Black as He's Painted* calls upon Alleyn to protect his friend, the Boomer, from an assassination attempt when the latter makes a state visit to England. Besides disdaining all precautions arranged by the Special Branch, the President appears to deliberately jeopardize his safety when he arranges an elaborate entertainment at the Ng'ombwanan Embassy. In fact, while appearing to take no precautions, the President has planned a counter offensive. Through the manipulation of events that lead witnesses to believe he is the victim of a failed assassination attempt, the President covers up the murder of a disloyal subject. The illusion he offers his audience has been foreshadowed by the *trompe l'oeil* perspective of the embassy's grounds. Obviously, Marsh's knowledge of perspective and her knowledge of theatre are crucial in imagining the setting. Although the embassy is set on a small parcel of London ground, its setting suggests the grandeur of Versailles.

> Vistas had achieved a false perspective by
> planting on either side of the long pond--
> yew trees, tall in the foreground, diminishing
> in size until they ended in miniatures. The
> pond itself had been correspondingly shaped.
> It was wide where the trees were tall and
> narrowed throughout its length. The *trompe
> l'oeil* was startling....at the far end of the little
> lake a pavilion had been set up where the
> Boomer, the Ambassador and a small assort-
> ment of distinguished guests would assemble
> for an *al fresco* entertainment (4).

During the course of the entertainment, all lights are extinguished except for the lights in the pavilion where the President and his entourage sit opposite the lit stage where native drummers and Ng'ombwana's most famous singer perform. Marsh markedly equates the spectacle of the President with that of the performers on stage at the other end of the garden. Both enjoy the spotlight and at the crucial moment, "the President and the singer, at opposite ends of the lake, were the only persons to be seen in the benighted garden" (5). The former British ambassador remarks that "[t]he stage management, as one feels inclined to call it...is superb," (6). Furthermore, Marsh deliciously suggests the true nature of the event by accompanying the President's entrance with a song, "With a Little Bit of Luck" from a contemporary musical comedy. Alleyn forms part of the audience for the killing, as he does for the later ritualistic questioning of the spear thrower who brought the ambassador down. Throughout the rest of the novel, Alleyn tests his knowledge of the Boomer's character against the possibility that the Boomer's behavior is a calculated performance.

Another performance, one that reveals the identity of a murderer, anticlimactic a revelation as it may be, takes place in Marsh's novel, *Last Ditch*. In this novel, Ricky Alleyn, now grown up, has retreated to a Channel issland in order to explore his talent as a writer and his ability to complete a first novel. In addition to the usual difficulties inherent in a writer's task, Ricky's attempts to work are interrupted by a series of distractions. He falls in love; he unwittingly stumbles on the local branch of an international drug ring; and he gets caught up in speculations about a local young woman's murder. Although the action appears to link the drug dealing and the murder, the hypothetical link is a red herring. The murder is committed by Mr. Harkness, the girl's uncle, whose religious fanaticism has unbalanced him. This same fanaticism compels him to invite the island's inhabitants to a religious service where he plans to reveal everyone's sins, including his own.

The performance dramatizes his skewed perception of the lives around him. His use of biblical rhetoric to describe their lives encourages some members of his audience to think of his presentation as a performance best described in biblical and theatrical terms. Mr. Harkness appears on a platform in the back of his barn which serves as a hall. His entrance was

"...a star entrance and if Mr. Harkness had been an actor he would have been accorded a round of applause" (7). The heavens open and the rain pours down almost drowning out the climax of his speech which has been building to his confession. Alleyn thinks afterward that "[o]ne might be forgiven...for supposing that some celestial stage manager had taken charge, decided to give Mr. Harkness the full treatment, and grossly overdone it" (8). Since they are in the audience, Alleyn and Fox are witnesses to Harkness's startling retreat into an inner room where he hangs himself. Another character later refers to these events as the storm scene, as she "...expect[s] it would be called in Shakespeare" (9).

Many of Alleyn's cases which involve illicit drug dealing present Marsh with excellent opportunities to describe the false fronts of suspected criminals. In many ways, *Last Ditch* is a rewriting of an earlier work, *Spinsters in Jeopardy* in which the child Ricky becomes the kidnap victim of members of a drug distribution ring who pose as members of a religious cult. New members attracted to the cult of The Children of the Sun, often wealthy heiresses, soon become addicted to the drugs slipped into their cigarette tobacco. To the Alleyns who arrive at the Château de la Chèvre d'Argent, the evil underpinnings of the pseudo-religion are no surprise. Alleyn, sent to the French Mediterranean town of Roqueville to investigate the drug ring, immediately marks the suspicious nature of this group.

> ...there's nothing so very unusual about the
> religio-erotic racket....The cult of the Child-
> ren of the Sun in the Outer is merely a useful
> sideline and a means, I suspect, of gratifying
> a particularly nasty personal taste...The Sûreté
> is interested in the narcotics side of the show
> and Yard's watching it from our end (10).

Alleyn defines his role as a link between the two official groups, but he also investigates his impression that a murder has been committed under cover of the charade known as the Thursday night ritual. In order to gather evidence and prevent another murder, Alleyn and a French assistant infiltrate these rites by wearing hooded costumes and replacing two members of the group. When Alleyn crosses over the doorstep to the hidden temple chamber, he feels that he has entered a distorted reflection of the real world, as if "everyday objects had begun to change their values" (11). Sharing the perceptions of the drugged cult members, he enters into a staged setting to watch a performance complete with costumes, lighting, music, and special effects. Five daggers drop from the ceiling; car batteries and flash powder produce a blaze of light; fluorescent paint illuminates a bleating goat. Troy had compared a similar scene to bad cinematography, and Alleyn finds this scene bad theatre--unconvincing. Later Alleyn realizes that the murder he viewed from his train compartment, like good theatre, was illusory but convincing. He had not seen the crime directly, but reflected in a mirror.

Alleyn had encountered a similar pseudo-religious/drug cult in the 1936 novel, *Death in Ecstasy*. When Alleyn's friend and transcriber, Nigel Bathgate, wanders into the House of the Sacred Flame out of curiosity one rainy evening, he joins a hypnotized · congregation in their unexpected observation of a murder during a ritual ceremony. Marsh uses the term "performance" at several points in the novel to emphasize the theatricality inherent in events. Images from Druid religion and Nordic myth create a bizarre and unconvincing background for the events that follow. When Bathgate joins the congregation, he notes a number of stage effects arranged to create an atmosphere to induce credulity. The church is in total darkness, but upon the entrance of the priest, red lights and an enormous flame spring out of the darkness. Above the altar burns the sanctuary flame "in all its naptha-like theatricality" (12). While the congregation watches, the inner circle of initiates passes around a chalice of wine and drinks from it until one of them writhes to the floor in a death agony. As he watches, Bathgate begins to feel that "There was something indecent about these performances" (13).

Alleyn soon learns that some of the initiates have backed the temple as an investment with a good return. He discovers that the priest has hooked several of the inner circle on drugs which are supplied by another member of the group who is a big-time drug trafficker. In this instance, Bathgate functions as a stand-in for Alleyn who does not witness the group's initial performance. Together with Fox and Bathgate, Alleyn does become part of the audience for its final performance, a boardroom discussion that is transmitted by hidden microphones. The case ends in the "dramatic close" Alleyn most enjoys (14) as the police rush in and handcuff the murderer just as he gets ready to kill again. Several of the initiates react strongly to this denouement: "Mrs. Candour, seconded by Claude and Lionel, screamed steadily throughout this performance..." (15). This case, like the others discussed above, points out Alleyn's function as an audience to criminal performances. Marsh's detective is always aware of the construction of crime as an aesthetic act. He is always looking at the suspects and determining which are playing "roles," as he tries to catch them in that one moment when they step out of character. In this novel, the murderer slips once when using the Australian term "good oh," since he presents himself as an American entrepreneur. Alleyn picks up immediately on this slip of the tongue.

Death of a Fool is probably Marsh's quintessential novel of those centered around theatrical performances

outside the theatre setting. Here the key elements of many of
Marsh's novels are present: a theatre-like spectacle, the
presentation of crime as acting, and the emphasis on Alleyn as
an observer/audience. The theatrical elements of nontheatre
settings appearing separately in various Marsh novels come
together in this work, just as the elements found independently
in various Sword Dance celebrations in different English
villages all appear in the spectacle at the heart of the novel, the
South Mardian Sword Dance and Play. The novel exhibits a
murder during a spectacle, characters connected to the
theatre, a demonstration of Alleyn's and other characters'
knowledge of Shakespeare, the framing of action in theatrical
metaphors, and a reconstruction of the events leading to
murder. In his comments to Fox, Alleyn characterizes the
case as Elizabethan theatre:

> This case smacks of the Elizabethan. And I
> don't altogether mean *Hamlet* or *Lear*. Or
> ninemen's morris, though there's a flavour of
> all of them, to be sure. But those earlier plays
> of violence when people kill each other on a
> sort of quintessence of spleen and other people
> cheer each other up by saying things like, 'And
> now, my lord, to leave these doleful dumps' (16).

Alleyn is beginning to envision the village as a doleful dump,
but he can't leave until he solves the paradox of the crime: no
one could have committed it, but someone did.

The murdered man's granddaughter, Camilla Campion,
student at the Royal Academy, equates the sword dance with
a theatrical performance when she wishes her grandfather
good luck with his rehearsal. Her comment when he insists he
is going to a practice indicates that both are the same thing.
Later, she can remember clearly the movement of the dancers

because "One looked at it in terms of theatre" (17). Her evaluation of one of the performers praises him because he "...does get pretty well into the skin of that character" (18). The local doctor who aids Alleyn with the case also connects the fertility festival and the theatre when he views the dance as the highest manifestation of *King Lear*.

When the novel opens, the village of South Mardian lies isolated by heavy snow and the severe cold temperatures that have arrived just prior to the Winter Solstice. The weather that distances the village from the outside world makes it the perfect location for the performance of the Mardian Sword Dance, an authentic folk ritual passed down intact from father to son by the Andersen family at the forge. This authenticity reincarnates the past for the present audience of villagers and a local aristocratic family. The highlight of the ritual is the Dance of the Five Sons performed every year by the Andersen family and several other villagers. The Fool, an old man's role, is played by "The Guiser" as the eldest Andersen is called. His five sons play the five sons in the dance. The local doctor plays the traditional music on his fiddle, while the great grandson of the Dame at Mardian Castle plays the traditional male-female character known as the Betty, and Simon Begg, another villager, plays the part of the Hobby Horse. The traditional fertility celebration comes to an abrupt halt when the dancers discover that the Fool, who dies but returns to life in the ceremony, really has been beheaded behind the stone doleman. With fifty villagers and the Mardian family looking on, no one saw the murder. No one could have gone behind the stone without being seen, and the Guiser could not have left his place without being observed. Somehow the murder was committed during the course of the play, but there are no witnesses despite a large audience. Events strike observers as the phenomena of illusion turning into reality. As Alleyn remarks, the murder is so inexplicable that in an earlier age, the murder would have been credited to magic or supernatural causes.

Because the case is "lousy with motive" (19), Alleyn decides that he must establish who had the opportunity to kill. As in *Enter a Murderer* and *The Nursing Home Murder*, Alleyn decides to hold a reconstruction of the crime. Usually at the end of each novel, Alleyn reconstructs the crime verbally either for himself or for an audience of suspects or policemen. An actual reconstruction goes one step beyond that and allows him to call to mind details he has forgotten or to see for himself the individuals' movements when they repeat their performances. In *Death of a Fool*, a reconstruction also gives Alleyn an opportunity to manipulate events to force some of the suspects to reveal the parts of their accounts they have suppressed. Like a director, he intervenes in the unfolding of events in order to make sense of some of the testimony he has recorded.

During the actual performance, one of the performers, Begg, left the stage and let a German folklore fanatic named Mrs. Bünz wear his costume and take his place. This deception, crucial to the commission of the murder, succeeded because the costume conceals the wearer's identity. Mrs. Bünz had denied leaving the audience but when Alleyn stops the reconstruction and questions her mercilessly, she admits her hidden participation although not the actual course of events that followed. Alleyn relies on shock tactics to reveal those events. In the reconstruction, Alleyn arranges for the dead man's grandson to play his role without informing the rest of the players that the Guiser's part has been filled. The grandson appears as a disconcerting ghost-like white figure. He follows Alleyn's instructions to grab Mrs. Bünz's legs when she steps over him in the Hobby Horse costume and demonstrates how the Guiser was pulled off stage while under this costume. Murdered offstage by another suspect, he was later smuggled back to his original position under the same costume worn by a different character. Thus, *Death of a Fool* displays a brilliant use of a favorite Marsh ploy of a play within a play. Like the play in *Hamlet*, Alleyn's favorite drama, the reconstruction reveals a murder and the identity of a murderer to a watching audience.

As in other of Marsh's mysteries, the performance is not gratuitous to the structure of the novel, but encapsulates the tensions that underlie the fictional world of the novel. In *A Wreath for Rivera*, the scripting of the musical performance reflects the offstage balance of power between the band leader, a crazy peer, and the band members. In *Colour Scheme*, the performance delineates the relationships between the Maoris and the settlers of British descent. In *Black as He's Painted*, the spectacle brings to a climax the elaborate political counterplotting of the Ng'ombwanan President. *Death of a Fool* offers a spectacle that sums up the generational struggles underpinning daily village life. Each character in the play exists outside the play as well. The Dance of the Five Sons is danced by William Andersen's five sons Daniel, Andrew, Nathaniel, Christopher, and Ernest and the Guiser is referred to as an old fool. Because of his epilepsy, Ernie also doubles as a fool, and his motive for murder stems from his desire to dance the part of the Fool. The double of the promiscuous Betty character of the play is the generous Trixie, the beautiful and amoral barmaid. The phallic hobby horse character calls to mind Trixie's former lover, the amorous Ralph Stayne, called a "rake" by his aunt and "a proper man" by Trixie. The old Guiser represents both the preserver of tradition and the impediment to change since he blocked the engagements of his son Chris to Trixie and his granddaughter Camilla to Ralph. The Guiser also opposed plans to bring his business up-to-date by converting the forge into a gas station. Therefore, his death removes obstacles from the lovers' paths and frees his sons to make their own plans. Although his murder prevents the Fool's resurrection scene in the original dance, his grandson's performance in the reconstruction suggests a resurrection where age is replaced by youth. The comedic ending of marriage between the two young lovers, Camilla and Ralph, also suggests renewal and regeneration. Alleyn identifies the source of the "morris dance--cum sword dance--cum mumming play" as a religious mystery play when he discusses it with Dr. Otterly: "The ritual death of the Fool is the old mystery of sacrifice, isn't it, with the promise of renewal behind it?" (20). Thus he connects religious mysteries with modern mysteries.

Even the outsider, Mrs. Bünz, recreates in the dance the role she plays in the village of an outsider and a watcher who zealously seeks hidden information. She wants to document this relatively unspoiled version of folk ritual, but no one willingly gives her information about it. To supplement the few scraps of information they let drop, she decides to spy on the dance's participants. During their rehearsals in the unused barn behind the pub where she stays, she stands in the freezing cold and watches the rehearsal through a dirty window. Alleyn later sees her footprints frozen in the snow, deduces her behavior and from it, the extent of her zeal. He then concludes that she had also taken part in the ceremony by hiding under the costume of the Hobby. Her close observation of the dance explains her ability to recount many of its steps and movements as well as her quotation of the Guiser's dialogue that few people knew. Alleyn can understand her zeal and dedication as a watcher because her behavior typifies his own central function in his detective work. He watches, observes, records, tries to fill in the gaps, and often needs to gain entry into a relatively close knit group of suspects while camouflaging his purpose.

As Alan J. and Linda J. Dooley have pointed out, in Marsh's fiction, "the occupants of [her] fictional worlds tend to be closed groups that are bound together and are also...isolated from the rest of the world" (21). The fictional structure that introduces Alleyn to characters belonging to various groups ingeniously recreates the country house murder formula in a variety of milieux. Alleyn is very comfortable in the world of the theatre, as Bargainnier notes, and this setting with its company of actors reappears frequently in Marsh's fiction (22). Other groups include artists (in which the character of Alleyn's wife Troy serves as a connection), villagers, aristocrats, drug rings, religious cults, residents of a particular location such as a household or a spa, a group of travelers, and a hospital staff. In two novels when he works as an undercover agent, Alleyn hides either his name or his profession, but usually he appears openly in his professional capacity. Alleyn relies on interviews, psychological knowledge of the suspects, and knowledge of individuals' movements to solve crimes. Therefore, in the process of collecting information, Alleyn must have access to information that suspects would be hesitant to reveal to a policeman particularly when the charge will be murder. He is an observer, but he also needs access to the knowledge of the group members. Sometimes he maintains a hidden presence in the group, such as when he dresses in costume or uses a hidden microphone. At other times he may use a proxy like Nigel Bathgate who can be invited into suspects' apartments as happened in *Death in Ecstasy*; Trixie, the maid who can observe Mrs. Bünz's bruised shoulders; or a policeman who like Obby is keeping "obo" by guarding the Andersen brothers. The most amusing example of this latter situation must be the assignment of P. C. Martin to guard the riotous Lamprey family in *Death of a Peer*. In order to bar his access to their communication, they chatter away in French while their words are accurately recorded by Martin who had done military service in France and knows the language. Unknown to them, Alleyn has the advantage of being able to compare their uninhibited private conversation with the version of events they give him. Mrs. Lamprey is sure she has successfully misled Alleyn in his attempt to identify which twin was in the elevator with his dead uncle. In her misplaced confidence she assures her family that Alleyn "hasn't the faintest idea of what I was up to. Don't worry. Soyez tranquil" (23). Martin faithfully records "Soyez tranquil." Alleyn, of course, has been doing some acting of his own and was not as taken in as it seemed.

The Lampreys are typical of many of the aristocracy who are overjoyed to think that the investigating policeman is one of their own kind. Mrs. Lamprey reacts very typically when she tries to find out if they are in any way related. Dame Alice Mardian had done the same when she consulted a reference work on the peerage in order to find kinship with a maternal great aunt of Alleyn's. Of course, Dame Alice is never a suspect and her support of Alleyn makes his investigation easier. In *Scales of Justice*, Lady Hermione Lacklander calls through to the Yard to request that the son of her friend, Lady Alleyn, be assigned to the case because "[i]n the circumstances,...[she] prefers to deal with a gent" (24). Actually, she prefers not to have a disgraceful episode of her dead husband's career come to light and feels she can rely on the bond of class to avoid the scrutiny of the police. She also needs to conceal her son's rather stupid and unchivalrous behavior. Alleyn pointedly draws the line between them when he informs Lady Lacklander that she may call him Roderick, but only when they are alone together. He knows that the Lacklanders believe they can outwit him, but while he plays the role they expect, he gathers damaging information against them. They realize later that their social status is not enough to grant them special privilege in regard to telling the truth. To Lady Lacklander, this realization comes as a shock:

> Her face was too fat to be expressive. She
> seemed merely to stare at Alleyn in a meditative
> fashion, but she had gone very pale. At last she
> said without moving, "George, it's time to tell
> the truth" (25).

The confusion about Alleyn's status in a group reappears again in *Last Ditch*. The Pharamond family members are main characters. Alleyn and Troy met them during a cruise, and their son Ricky becomes friendly with Julia and Jasper Pharamond when he arrives on the Channel island where they live. When Alleyn appears later in the novel, he suspects a family member of being high up in the drug ring. Louis Pharamond, a prime suspect, has disappeared. When the family turns to Alleyn for help and information, Jasper Pharamond finally realizes the need to guard their remarks because they are talking to a policeman. Alleyn explains to them that he is in a situation that poses a problem, at least for him. Since the police now want Louis for questioning, his position precludes his sharing the information they request. Julia aptly characterizes the situation in her final remark. "And we actually asked you to come and help us...It's like the flies asking the spider to walk into their parlor" (26).

The line blurs even more in *Death in a White Tie* when Alleyn observes London high society in order to uncover a blackmailer and a murderer. He personally knows many of the protagonists which gives him an advantage but also involves him more emotionally than usual. In order to track a blackmailer he convinces his old friend Lord Robert "Bunchy" Gospell to go undercover for him and observe the movements of potential candidates. When Bunchy is murdered, Alleyn vows to track down the murderer even if it takes his whole life, costs him his job, or means that he will need to kill the murderer himself. Alleyn's outburst stems from feeling for his friend, but his reaction makes clear that he surveys the suspects and secrets of the upper class with the same determination he applies to all his cases. His class may claim him, but he does not claim it. He has left the diplomatic service for police work which members of his class suggest is an unusual profession for the son of a peer. Alleyn is a member of the aristocracy, but he has rejected full membership by his choice of profession and the tempering of his class loyalty. Instead of sustaining the upper class's vision of itself, he scrutinizes and tests the behavior of its members as he does the suspects of all classes. Whether his suspects are aristocrats or not, Alleyn occupies a pivotal position as watcher/audience and simultaneously, a figure who is accorded the privilege of access to the inner workings of the observed group.

The duality of his position closely parallels the double nature of Marsh's experience as a colonial writer who divided her time and life between two continents and two careers. In the late 1920's, Marsh was able to make the first of many trips to England where she joined her friends, the Rhodes family, who served as models for the Lampreys. After prolonging her stay and trying out a variety of ways to earn a living, Marsh wrote her first detective novel, *A Man Lay Dead* (1934). Following her return to New Zealand in 1932, Marsh's life developed the pattern that characterized her long career. In New Zealand, her detective fiction was rarely mentioned by her friends, who Marsh claimed were motivated by tactfulness. Instead of recognition for her writing, Marsh's life in New Zealand won her the reputation of an outstanding director, particularly of Shakespearean drama. Although New Zealand had no professional repertory company, Marsh's work with the student players at the University of Canterbury at Christchurch won her deserved recognition, and many actors she trained acknowledged her talent when they became professionals. In England where she returned at frequent intervals, Marsh was recognized primarily as a writer of outstanding detective fiction. Marsh loved her home in New Zealand but needed frequent trips to England to keep in touch with the material for her fiction and to reinvigorate her life by an intense absorption into a stimulating cultural climate. Margaret Lewis, Marsh's recent biographer, argues that Marsh's visits to England allowed her to adopt the privileged position of an observer. She quotes Marsh on her awareness of the nature of her position in relation to her English friends:

> It's the difference between, say, being in a
> talking picture and looking at it...I'm in the
> position now where I look at the talking
> picture but I've also made friends with the
> actors in it. But I'm not yet completely part
> of the cast in the film, I think...I couldn't
> bear to think that I wasn't coming back
> every three or four years (27).

Lewis believes that the detective formula "provided exactly the right framework for a stylized view of life that would shed no light on the writer's much valued privacy" (28). Yet the novels do make clear the emotions coloring their author's frame of mind, for the character of her detective also experiences the dual relation to others of observer and confidant. Marsh's simultaneous experience of connection and dislocation shape the relationships between her detective and the other characters in her novels.

In addition, Alleyn's reaction to the characters of two young New Zealanders introduced to the London metropolis also reflected Marsh's position after her arrival. In the 1940 novel, *Death of a Peer*, the young New Zealander Roberta Grey arrives to visit the Lamprey family. Since Marsh modeled the Lampreys on her friends whom she met in New Zealand before their return to England, she included many autobiographical elements. Roberta Grey's relationship with the Lampreys resembles Marsh's own relationship with the Rhodes. Both are observers as well as devoted friends. Roberta participates with her friends in the charade presented to entertain Lord Wutherwood just before he is murdered in the elevator as he is about to depart. Her allegiance is to the family, yet she has a very clear view of their behavior that does not minimize their faults. After the murder she feels that they have been completely withdrawn from her and arranged matters between themselves. Her outsider status is reinforced by her inability to speak French, the medium the family uses to communicate their strategy. Roberta goes as far as to lie to Alleyn, but she is a poor and unconvincing actress. Alleyn admires her, though, for her courage and loyalty. Eventually, her testimony helps Alleyn break the case and her view of the family convinces the young Henry Lamprey to abandon the extravagant Lamprey ways and look for a job. Another young New Zealander who arrives in London to find work is Martyn Tarne. In the novel *Night at the Vulcan*, Martyn realizes the dream of every aspiring actor that an unknown player can step into an important role when fortune throws it her way. She arrives penniless, with no obvious connections, but like Marsh herself experiences success. Beginning as a dresser and ending as an actress, her relationship to the troupe emphasizes that she is an outsider and an observer. Here again, Alleyn establishes a special connection with her that pays off by rewarding him with the information that allows Alleyn to solve the case. Tarne, like Grey, forms a connecting link between Alleyn and a group to which he does not belong. The New Zealanders' observations are valuable to him because these characters are not truly part of the group they describe and therefore they offer objective assessments.

Marsh may have deliberately employed reticence in her autobiography, even when rewriting the slightly more personal later version. Yet readers of her many detective novels will find enough clues to deduce some of her concerns. Her use of her theatrical knowledge to construct her detective fiction demonstrates that Marsh suggests a strong comparison between stage performances and the criminal performances in her work. Although in life her careers as theatrical director and a writer of detective fiction remained separated, in her fiction she brought these two interests together. In doing so, she created a detective hero who suggested her own sense of living a dual existence. Marsh's readers can view her fiction as an artistic performance that reveals her response as a colonial writer who loved equally her native country and the country of her English ancestors.

ENDNOTES

1. Margaret Lewis, *Ngaio Marsh: A Life* (London: Clio Press, 1992), 80.
2. T. Todorov, "The Typology of Detective Fiction," in *Modern Criticism and Theory*, ed. David Lodge (New York: Longman, 1988), 158-65.
3. Todorov, 160.
4. Ngaio Marsh, *Black as He's Painted* (New York: Jove Books, 1981), 62; hereafter cited as *BHP*.
5. Marsh, *BHP*, 79.

6. Marsh, *BHP*, 77.
7. Ngaio Marsh, *Last Ditch* (Boston: Little, Brown and Company, 1977), 238; hereafter cited as *LD*.
8. Marsh, *LD*, 240.
9. Marsh, *LD*, 243.
10. Ngaio Marsh, *Spinsters in Jeopardy* (New York: Berkley Publishing, 1978), 60; hereafter cited as *SJ*.
11. Marsh, *SJ*, 225.
12. Ngaio Marsh, *Death in Ecstasy* (London: Geoffrey Bles, 1936), 9; hereafter cited as *DE*.
13. Marsh, *DE*, 11.
14. Marsh, *DE*, 233.
15. Marsh, *DE*, 233.
16. Ngaio Marsh, *Death of a Fool* (New York: Jove Books, 1978), 243; hereafter cited as *DF*.
17. Marsh, *DF*, 142.
18. Marsh, *DF*, 140.
19. Marsh, *DF*, 198.
20. Marsh, *DF*, 118.
21. Allan J. and Linda J. Dooley, "Rereading Ngaio Marsh," *Art in Crime Writing: Essays on Detective Fiction*, ed. Bernard Benstock (New York: St. Martin's Press, 1983), 33-48.
22. Earl F. Bargainnier, "Ngaio Marsh's 'Theatrical' Murders," *The Armchair Detective*, 10 (April 1977), 175-81.
23. Ngaio Marsh, *Death of a Peer* (New York: Berkley, 1994), 190.
24. Ngaio Marsh, *Scales of Justice* (New York: Jove Books, 1980), 67.
25. Marsh, *SJ*, 235.
26. Marsh, *LD*, 215.
27. Lewis, 95.
28. Lewis, 88.

Ode on a Favorite Novel--
Drowned in a Sea of Memory

by Catherine Aird

It has been my experience that there are few pleasures in life to equal the one which is now and then--but never often enough, of course--relished by the devoted reader of the works of a much loved author: namely the peculiar thrill enjoyed on the publication of a good new book by a good old author.

There are--alas--even fewer pleasures in advancing beyond middle age, but I have found that one of them is being able to recreate this singular enjoyment after an interval of very nearly thirty years by rereading Ngaio Marsh's *Death at the Dolphin* (1966).

I am happy to say that I can still conjure up a clear recollection of reading it for the first time when this volume was originally published in 1967 in the United Kingdom by Messrs William Collins. It had come out in the United States the previous year under the imprint of Little, Brown of Boston with the title *Killer Dolphin*.

By that year I had read Ngaio Marsh's complete detective fiction *oeuvre* to date and I had come across her works beginning, quite fortuitously, I remember, with *Death and the Dancing Footman* (1942). I had encountered that book in the memorably heady days following my graduation from the juvenile section of our local public library

(I may say that experiencing no other rite of passage before or since has made such a mark on my consciousness.)

Oddly enough, though, for some reason too deep and difficult to identify--but nevertheless there--the reading of an old title not hitherto encountered does not come into quite the same category as the reading of a new one by the same favorite author. This might of course be because "everyone else" (well, other readers, anyway) has already read it, and one is merely catching up with earlier aficionados which is not the same. We all want to be the first to know. (The exception that proves this rule must surely be John Keats's excitement in "On First Looking into Chapman's Homer.")

On the other hand it could be that we are all spiritual brothers of those comprising the crowd on the pier at New York who cried out to the passengers on the transatlantic packet steamer approaching with the latest installment of Charles Dickens's serial *The Old Curiosity Shop* on board, "Did Little Nell die?" We none of us want to be the last to know either.

Death at the Dolphin first made its impact on me in 1967 even before I reached the beginning of the narrative, and I found myself stirred again when I re-read the dedication. This is to Edmund Cork "in gratitude and with affection." Edmund Cork, doyen of the famous firm of Messrs Hughes, Massie Ltd., was Ngaio Marsh's literary agent and had just then also become my literary agent. I, too, was in the subsequent years to echo and endorse her gratitude and affection both to Edmund Cork and his heirs and successors.

What I did not know then and do know now was that Ngaio Marsh was coming up to seventy-three years of age when she wrote *Death at the Dolphin*--certainly in my view one of her most accomplished novels. There is a great confidence about the whole plot and a very skilled hand patently at work on the theme and background. It therefore comes as no surprise to learn from Margaret Lewis's biography that this book was no longer in the making than usual for the author and was the better for it (1).

Ngaio Marsh's own autobiography *Black Beech and Honeydew* had already been published in 1965 and, interestingly, contains no specific reference to this book on which she must even then have begun to work but, most significantly, there is an account of her visit many years before with Tyrone Guthrie and others to a severely bomb-damaged theatre in Woolwich (2). This was to see if it would be suitable for a Shakespearean production in the Festival of Britain in 1951. It was not good for Tyrone Guthrie's purposes, but fifteen years or so later it was very good for the plot and setting of *Death at the Dolphin*.

Idly toying with literary titles that might have epitomized Ngaio Marsh and her work at this age, I discarded in turn Muriel Spark's *The Prime of Miss Jean Brodie*, Angus Wilson's *The Middle Age of Mrs Eliot*, and John Betjeman's *A Few Late Chrysanthemums*. This book is no late chrysanthemum and most women of seventy-three are reckoned to have passed both their prime and their middle-age, let alone their biblical allotted span. The word that comes most readily to mind is "veteran" although even that implies staying-power rather than the freshness which in my view this book has. "Top of her form" was how the critics of the day judged it (3).

Perhaps the best description of all of the doughty author at this stage of her life might be "Old Stager" since this book is of the theatre and is set firmly in it by a writer who knew her subject very well indeed. The Dolphin Theatre is a theatre which began in the story by being "dark" in the theatrical sense of the word and ended by being dark in the sense that has more to do with the world of darkness: the Muse of Tragedy, Melpomene, being a great deal more in evidence than her Sister of Comedy, Thalia.

This deep knowledge of the theatre on the author's part permeates the whole book--plot, line, and good (old) red herring. The subtle hand of a master craftsman can be seen at work especially in her use of the *dramatis personae* of the play as a device to introduce the reader to many of the members of the cast of the murder story, and similarly in her application of that age-old concept of "the play within the play."

This particular sub-plot has, of course, a very distinguished predecessor in *Hamlet* itself. Indeed the Shakespearean connection suffuses the main plot in more ways than one, the fictional dramatist of the book saying that he isn't the first "to have a bash at the man from Warwickshire" and he won't be the last (4).

Ngaio Marsh was not the first (nor, I am sure, will she be the last either) to invoke as she did an artifact from Stratford-upon-Avon in detective fiction. Edmund Crispin's *Love Lies Bleeding* (Gollancz, 1948) is a case in point, the supposed missing manuscript of Shakespeare's *Love's Labours Won* being the *casus belli* of that narrative.

In *Death at the Dolphin* it is a child's glove--not that of any child, naturally, and not any glove either--but a glove supposed to have been made by William Shakespeare's father for William Shakespeare's son--the poor young Hamnet. The boy had died young and his sad early demise, while not altering the course of history, had undoubtedly had its effect on English literature in that it was after Hamnet's death that most of the great tragedies flowed from his playwright father's pen. Ngaio Marsh paid her readers a subtle compliment without amplifying the statement by explaining that cheverel is the skin of a kid (5).

Marsh was also a member of a long and distinguished crime-writing tradition in finding the theatre--both amateur and professional--a good setting for a plot. Edmund Crispin had already set two other of his works in that arena; Margaret Erskine, Simon Nash, and J. S. Fletcher were also among those who had gone before. Those on the list of her contemporaries and successors in this respect are equally, if not more, well-known and include such famous names as P. D. James, Antonia Fraser, Ellis Peters, and Sara Woods.

The theatre and the play within the play have all the advantages of a closed setting and we, too, the readers, see the action through the proscenium arch, neatly taking in *en passant* the Aristotlean unities of time and place. There are other advantages as well in that the characters are disguised in the two senses that actors are rather than the more usual one-- without its in any way seeming contrived. The author herself says that actors make splendid copy and good material for detective fiction (6).

With Ngaio Marsh's personal expertise of the theatrical milieu we also see into the workings of the Green Room where the cast behave in and out of character at will, when a great deal more percipience is required on the part of the reader, and the writer skillfully performs what might be called a double act. Charles Random, one of the actor-characters in the book, actually apologizes when off-stage for "talking inside the play" (7).

The stage is not the only ingredient in the book. There is the important and tantalizing role of the mysterious Mr. Vassily Conducis who comes from somewhere between the Orient and the Occident and who is possessed of the untold wealth necessary to restore the ancient, neglected, and bomb-damaged theatre in and around which the plot is centered, although exactly why he did any such thing is almost the last mystery to be revealed. The reader is aware that the ravages of war were still around then--one character exhibiting "all the repose of an unexploded land mine" (8).

A great deal has been written about the novels of the Golden Age being social markers of their time, although Ngaio Marsh is not often included among those who have painted important word-pictures of their days, and I am sure would have had no pretensions as a social historian. Nevertheless there are one or two similes and phrases in *Death at the Dolphin* that might be cited as describing times that will not come again--a reference to a "gold albert" for instance. There will soon be--perhaps there are already--some who do not know that "a gold albert" is a type of watch (9); and there must be those in these days of clean air acts, smokeless fuel, and banned bonfires who have never "heard the fire settle" (10). To hear the fire settle will one day be an archaism, too, needing explanation in the same way as does "stapping someone's vitals."

There is a nice note, too, for those who may have forgotten how far censorship has been relaxed in the last thirty years, when a character in the book remarks, "...only the Lord Chamberlain stands between me and untold affluence" (11). On the other hand Superintendent Roderick Alleyn's observing to Br'er Fox, "I see you are in merry pin," (12) must have been more than a little old hat (if I may be forgiven the pun) even in 1967. Calling false teeth "china-boys" (13) is probably older still! In years to come the line, "We have got a story to make the front pages wish they were double elephants," will need a conscientious footnote about pre-decimal Imperial paper sizes (14).

As a writer Ngaio Marsh herself is not much drawn to the punning mode, but there is one rather nice theatrical in-joke put into the mouth of an actor/character. "Method in her madness. Or is it,...madness in her Method?" "That will do, Harry," says someone else--and it does (15).

Some phrases are surely pure Ngaio Marsh, and very good they are too: "Dearboymanship" is completely self-explanatory, bringing the informal world of the theatre to mind upon the instant (16). There is a lovely metaphor, though, which is as apt today as it was the day it was written when the press is described as being "in full lurk outside the theatre" (17). An "insistence of church bells" is delightfully evocative, too (18).

There are delicious shades of Noel Coward's song "Don't Put Your Daughter on the Stage, Mrs. Worthington" when the author writes of "the deadly knowingness of the professional mum" (19), of many a theatrical party in "Everybody was now obliged scream if he or she wished to be heard and almost everybody would have been glad to sit down" (20), and of the exclusively masculine world of the Masons when it is said of the female character, "She'd woo the Grand Master to let the goat out of the Lodge" (21).

There are profundities, too, and in places unexpected in a detective story, especially where the theatre is concerned. It is often dangerous to ascribe to authors the sentiments expressed by their characters in the course of the action of the plot but, if nothing more, it must mean that they have thought about what has been written. For instance: "Power corrupts,...didn't somebody say? It may do: but it comes in handy, dear boy, it comes in handy" (22).

The author writes very perceptively, too, for instance, about genius and finds it "nearly always slightly lacking in taste." "Talent," remarks one of her characters, again with great awareness, "only fluctuates about its own middle line whereas genius nearly always makes great walloping bloomers" (23). (Superintendent Alleyn said, "Murder's a crime in bad taste" (24) and promptly apologized for making the remark but that was rather different.)

I admit therefore to pure speculation--and may be wrong--in thinking I have found Ngaio Marsh's own credo in her summation in the last few paragraphs of this book. It is in the voice of an important character in the story, who is caused to say, "If you belong to the theatre,...you belong utterly" (25).

There is an old saying with a lot of wisdom in it that runs "the nuts come when the teeth are gone." I think they came in time for Ngaio Marsh.

ENDNOTES

1. Margaret Lewis, *Ngaio Marsh: A Life* (London: Chatto & Windus, 1991), 186.
2. Ngaio Marsh, *Black Beech and Honeydew* (London: Collins, 1965; rev. ed. 1981), 230.
3. Ibid., 197.
4. Ngaio Marsh, *Death at the Dolphin* (New York: Berkley Publishing, 1971, 2nd printing) 81. All references taken from this edition, referred to hereafter as *DD*.
5. Ngaio Marsh, *DD*, 37.
6. Marsh, *Blackbeech and Honeydew*, 302.
7. Marsh, *DD*, 80.
8. Marsh, *DD*, 222.
9. Marsh, *DD*, 83.
10. Marsh, *DD*, 37.
11. Marsh, *DD*, 219.
12. Marsh, *DD*, 244.
13. Marsh, *DD*, 113.
14. Marsh, *DD*, 111.
15. Marsh, *DD*, 225.
16. Marsh, *DD*, 72; cf "oldboymanship," 312.
17. Marsh, *DD*, 197.
18. Marsh, *DD*, 209.

19. Marsh, *DD*, 92.
20. Marsh, *DD*, 90.
21. Marsh, *DD*, 288.
22. Marsh, *DD*, 351.
23. Marsh, *DD*, 118.
24. Marsh, *DD*, 266.
25. Marsh, *DD*, 352.

Detective Fiction:

A Mirror of Social History

Ngaio Marsh's London

by Alzina Stone Dale

In her autobiography, *Black Beech and Honeydew* (1965), Dame Ngaio Marsh wrote that, while growing up in New Zealand, not only had she always wanted to go "Home," but that "You may say it was a...romantic and unreal London...I conjured up..." (1). In 1960, having been "Home" many times, Marsh told the BBC (British Broadcasting Corporation) about catching that "London feeling"--a freshness of impact which she got each time she landed (2). While biographer Kathryne Slate McDorman recognized that Marsh was a "hybrid," Marsh's most recent biographer, Margaret Lewis, took Marsh's first remark at face value and insisted that the "London" seen in Marsh's mysteries is "entirely fictitious" (3). Lewis's judgment, however, is both inaccurate and anachronistic because Marsh's fictional London is a surprisingly good fit for the real place.

Lewis's judgment about Marsh's use of setting comes from Lewis's contradictory view of Marsh herself. While insisting that Marsh never questioned the social status quo, Lewis also says that in England Marsh was "the outsider who benefited from an entree to very high society..., yet kept a necessary sense of detachment" (4). It seems to have escaped Lewis that popular literature seldom addresses specific social agendas, but often gives its readers a surprisingly realistic portrait of the times.

As a result, Lewis attempts to limit the scope of Marsh's mysteries first by adopting the conventional wisdom that mysteries are "minor" works. Specifically, Lewis sees Marsh's work as no longer old-fashioned but, like vintage cars having the "timeless qualities that always go with sound craftsmanship and good style" (5). In a word, her mysteries are period pieces. Second, Lewis not only echoes W. H. Auden's famous dictum that mystery's "guilty vicarage" (or scene of the crime) is located in the Garden of Eden when she calls Marsh's stories "mythical," but she also follows the party line of critics like Julian Symons, who despise mysteries that do not deal with important social issues. Symons's "mean streets" agenda, imported from America, paradoxically has its roots in G. K. Chesterton's 1902 defense of the detective as an urban knight. It comes from Symons's not so secret wish that the British class system would wither away, taking with it all fictional lords and ladies. Lewis also damns Marsh's mysteries with faint praise because Marsh did not write the Great New Zealand Novel.

But in assessing Marsh's work, it is far more useful to be chronologically correct than to be politically correct. Neither affirmative action nor ethnic provincialism, for example, were popular in Marsh's day. Instead, as McDorman pointed out, Marsh wanted to help the United Kingdom and New Zealand understand one another. As it did for her contemporary Dorothy L. Sayers, the idea of the British Empire (Commonwealth) still had meaning for Marsh because they saw its gifts as cultural, and its contribution the great works of the English language. The truly remarkable fact of Dame Ngaio's multi-faceted career was that she managed to be a citizen of both worlds and her New Zealand work in Shakespearean theater was a successful attempt to fuse them. In staging her productions, Marsh's motives were very similar to Sayers's hope that her translation of Dante's *Divine Comedy* would transmit Western Civilization's values to the postwar world.

The same concerns--and values--appear in Marsh's mysteries. Lewis agrees that Marsh was a skillful observer and that by the time she began to write detective stories, Marsh was accustomed to "transposing experience into prose." But although Marsh's British gentry, Maoris, actors and New Zealand sheep farmers were based upon her personal experience, Lewis still accuses Marsh of both snobbish attitudes and a narrowness of vision.

Part of the problem comes from Lewis's failure to see that, at home in both settings, Marsh still retained her artist/observer's eye. As a result, she drew wonderful word pictures for her readers, many of whom were scattered to the ends of the earth, and for many of us who had been to neither place, Marsh "drew" both her beloved New Zealand--and London--on the map.

Perhaps it takes one colonial to know another. While working on a biography of G. K. Chesterton, I wrote to Ngaio Marsh in 1979 to find out if she had been initiated into the Detection Club by G. K. C. Chesterton had not been well and only presided at Detection Club meetings now and then.

Pleasantly and promptly Marsh wrote back that she had not become a full member until after World War II when she spent more time in England and could attend the "obligatory number of...dinners." But she described her amusement when she went to a pre-war initiation presided over by Dorothy L. Sayers in full academic regalia with all the "top practitioners of the time" like John Dickson Carr, John Rhode, and Freeman Wills Crofts, taking part. Marsh added that "...they all seemed rather elderly to be indulging in these capers but it was great fun meeting them" (6).

Emboldened by her friendliness, I impulsively wrote Marsh again and asked if she had ever been put in her place as a mere "colonial." I had experienced this treatment as an American college student in the early 1950's when I was a most unwelcome

representative of the New World Order. At the same time, I had
felt the uncanny pull of my Puritan ancestors as I watched
Elizabeth II open her first Parliament, knowing they might have
stood cheering Elizabeth I on the self-same street.

Again Marsh responded with charm and intuition, saying
that she had found that the postwar U. K. still "had a pretty solid
bank of conscious or unconscious class structure in everyday
life...[but it was]...by no means as stringent and clearly defined as
it used to be..." (7).

The same careful observation and recognition of the social
situation pervades her settings. While doing the research for
Mystery Readers Walking Guide: London, I actually walked
Marsh's London streets and found that Marsh's London was far
freer of fancy than that of her British contemporaries like Agatha
Christie and Margery Allingham, who specialized in atmosphere,
but very seldom used real places. I also discovered that many of
Marsh's specific locations were in the parts of London where she
herself had lived (8).

In some of her best mysteries, Marsh made setting itself
a character. This gave those stories the added dimension that
Dorothy L. Sayers called "particularity." For Sayers the use of
genuine, or genuine-sounding, details of time and place
established the "veracity" of the work for the reader. Real
streets, buildings, institutions, customs and conversation all
contributed to this goal.

Although Marsh stated that she began with "people in
their immediate situation with no more than the scantiest
framework for a plot," her very phrase, "their immediate
situation," is really another term for "place" because Marsh chose
people appropriate to that scene (9). In this way, Marsh was not
so very different from a latter-day mystery writer like P. D. James
for whom setting is crucial to character and plot development.

My Marsh street-walking helped me to recognize the
remarkable job she had done of making her London seem real.

For example, Lewis stated that *A Wreath for Rivera* (1949) was a "throwback" to pre-war London and not an accurate description of the grim postwar city. But Marsh placed the offices of *Harmony*, for which Edward Manx wrote theatrical reviews and for which his eccentric uncle--the Marquis of Pastern and Baggott--wrote an anonymous advice to the lovelorn column, at 5 Materfamilias Lane, London E.C. 2.

"One end of Materfamilias Lane had suffered a bomb and virtually disappeared, but the other stood intact, a narrow city street, with ancient buildings, a watery smell, dark entries and impenitent charm" (10). Her "Materfamilias Lane" was superimposed on the real Paternoster Row northwest of St. Paul's Cathedral, where, in the early 1950's wandering about with a prewar guidebook, I had seen Paternoster Row in ruins. With a single sentence, Marsh evoked the desolation I felt at seeing the destruction around St. Paul's.

Marsh's use of place in her London mysteries falls into two main categories: the theatrical and the autobiographical. Her most impressive theatrical tour de force was the pair *Killer Dolphin* (1966) and *Light Thickens* (1982) in which she "superimposed" Shakespearean London on the postwar London of Elizabeth II.

A year before *Killer Dolphin* came out, in *Black Beech and Honeydew*, Marsh had related that in 1950 she and Tyrone Guthrie and his wife went down river to much-bombed Woolwich to inspect a theatre they hoped to rehabilitate for the Festival of Britain. They picked up the keys of the theatre at a pub but the damage was too extensive, so Marsh rebuilt the theatre in her imagination near Shakespeare's Globe Theatre (11).

Killer Dolphin opens just east of Blackfriars Bridge where the Blackfriars Theatre once stood. Young director Peregrine Jay lived there in a flat on the top of a converted warehouse. Idly exploring the South Bank through a pair of field-glasses, he spotted the stage-house of the Dolphin Theatre and had an adventure hunting it down across the Thames on Bankside at the end of Wharfingers Lane.

By the time of Marsh's last mystery, *Light Thickens*, the Blackfriars warehouse has become a family residence for Jay, his actress wife Emily and sons. There on "a sunny May Sunday [as] sightseers' craft plied up and down the Thames on their trips to the Tower...[the] Jays with Alleyn were drinking their after-luncheon coffee on the terrace outside their house. Across the river the Dolphin...sparkled in the sunshine" (12). By the early 1980's when this mystery came out, there had been considerable gentrification of the Pool of London just west of the Tower, and both of P. D. James's detectives, Adam Dalgliesh and Cordelia Gray lived there in converted lofts as well.

Like these theatrical mysteries, primarily focused onstage in a locked room ambiance but requiring a convincing city backdrop, Marsh's autobiographical mysteries make use of historic London and the places she herself lived. The most detailed descriptions of London as Marsh knew it at two very different periods a generation apart occur in *A Surfeit of Lampreys* (1940) and *Black as He's Painted* (1973). Many of her other mysteries use real London places, believably drawn, from a Harley Street doctor's office to (old) Scotland Yard, but these two not only use London as a setting but as a character in the plot. Long before her autobiography came out, *A Surfeit of Lampreys* had lovingly detailed the "geographical and emotional" arrival of a colonial, while the postwar *Black as He's Painted* described Marsh's favorite neighborhood of Brompton with such careful detail that one can walk into her life.

In *A Surfeit of Lampreys*, Marsh's "fictional" London began at the Port of London across the Isle of Dogs from the East End, where the ships from New Zealand used to dock. New Zealander Roberta Grey overheard a passenger say, "'Good old Thames.' She heard names that were strange yet familiar: Gravesend, Tilbury, Greenhithe..." (13).

Henry and Frid Lamprey met her ship and took her west by cab to London proper, murmuring about Limehouse and Poplar as they went by. Roberta was only vaguely disappointed that the places were so much less romantic than their associations, which is certainly the fact. She was also too bemused to enjoy the fact that these seasoned Londoners constantly mixed up their "sights." Past the Tower they came to the City and Henry and Frid pointed uncertainly to the Mansion House and suggested she should look at the dome of St. Paul's. At Ludgate Hill, Henry said, "Here's Fleet Street...Do you remember 'Up the Hill of Ludgate, down the Hill of Fleet?'" knowing that for Roberta "real" London also existed in song and story (14).

Although frequenters of the theatre district around St. Martin's Lane, Marsh's characters rarely set foot in Bloomsbury, for their natural habitat was in the shops and galleries of Oxford and Bond Street and the mansions of Mayfair and Belgravia. But for colonials, the most important site in London was at the edge of the theatre district on the border between the West End and Soho: Piccadilly Circus.

As Henry pointed to Eros, Marsh wrote,

...to British colonials the symbol of London is...homely...a small figure perched slantways above a roundabout, an elegant Victorian god with a Grecian name--Eros of Piccadilly Circus...[they] orientate themselves by Piccadilly Circus. All their adventures start from there. It is under...Eros that to many a colonial has come that first warmth of realization that says... 'This is London.' It is here...that the colonial wakes from the trance of arrival[,] finds his feet on London paving stones[,] and is suddenly happy.

'It's not so big,' said Roberta.
'Quite small, really,' said Henry (15).

Marsh's characters rarely go to Westminster except to be interrogated at (old) Scotland Yard, the great striped tiger on the banks of the Thames across from No.10 Downing Street. But beyond Scotland Yard across Bridge Street is the clock tower with Big Ben, another symbol evocative of British influence. When Roberta Grey hears the boom, Henry says, "...Big Ben. You hear him all over the place at night time." "I've only heard him on the air before." "You're in London now" (16).

Alleyn was often at Scotland Yard late at night as he was on the evening of the Carrados's debut in *Death in a White Tie* (1938). "Out there in the cold, Big Ben tolled one...The row of lamps hung like a necklace of misty globes along...the Embankment," and Alleyn (sounding far more like colonial Marsh than a native Englishman) thought, "Fog in June...This England!" just as a scared cabby brought him the body of Lord Robert (Bunchy) Gospell (17).

To know Marsh's London intimately, one has to explore her Brompton, also known as Knightsbridge, the home of Harrods. This was Marsh's special territory from the time she first went to London, and reading about her visits there, it is clear that, like Sayers, Marsh used her own succession of flats as housing for her characters.

In the 1930's Marsh and her friend "Charlot Lamprey" opened a gift shop on the Brompton Road. Getting ready to help Charlot (Nelly Rhodes in real life) run the shop, Marsh lived at the large white Hotel Rembrandt across Brompton Road from the domed Brompton Oratory. But when they moved to a larger shop on Beauchamp Place, south of Brompton Road, it failed. Marsh and a student secretary later lived on Beauchamp Place during a 1950's visit.

Marsh's most famous flat was the basement off Sloane Square where she and her mother were living when one rainy Sunday in 1931, having finished reading a detective story, Marsh decided to write one herself. She had recently visited Dulwich College, her father's beloved alma mater, founded by a famous actor of Shakespeare's time, Edward Alleyn, so it seems inevitable that she named her detective "Alleyn" (18).

Much later in *Black as He's Painted*, Mr. Witherspoon, Marsh's most delightful civil servant (apart from Alleyn himself) a bored, retired Foreign Office official, wandered out of his dreary Hyde Park flat across the park and found himself in a Brompton adventure. Every step of Mr. Witherspoon's way can be traced, leading one straight to the place where he found himself following Lucy, a small cat, into a tiny neighborhood that Marsh renamed "the Capricorns."

The entrance to Capricorn Mews had an arch too low for any but pedestrian traffic. Inside it was "...narrow, orderly, sunny, with a view, to the left, of tree-tops and the dome of the Baronsgate Basilica" (19). The houses were small, well-kept Georgian and Victorian with iron railings; at one corner was a pub, the Sun in Splendour. In Marsh's masterly reconstruction there is also a Capricorn Walk and Street. Mr. Witherspoon surprised himself by buying 1 Capricorn Walk and adopting Lucy the cat, only to become mixed up in the murder at the Ng'ombwana embassy around the corner in Palace Park Gardens (really Princes Gardens on Exhibition Road).

Having read Marsh's autobiography and stared at the map, I headed straight down Brompton Road past Harrods where I found "the Montpeliers"--Montpelier Street, Montpelier Square, Montpelier Terrace, and Montpelier Walk. Marsh herself had lived in Montpelier Walk in "a little house...on the sunny side of the street looking towards the dome of the [Brompton] Oratory...." Marsh enjoyed Montpelier Square's decorous pub, "the Prince of Wales...in the foreground," and the row of nicely kept small terraces with tiny balconies and delicate ironwork railings (20).

This selection of factual-fictional sites in Brompton shows Marsh using her London as the setting for her fiction. Seen on foot as well as read about in her mysteries, these places certainly do not suggest a mythical city, unrecognizable by either its inhabitants or by the traveler. As Douglas G. Greene put it, "...[Marsh] born and reared far from England...brought to her writing the clearsightedness of an outsider--an outsider who could view a scene as a painter..." (21). Marsh's place settings were not only lovingly drawn by a master artist but are also still recognizably true to life.

ENDNOTES

1. Ngaio Marsh, *Black Beech and Honeydew* (London: Collins, 1965), 205; cited hereafter as *BBHD*.
2. Margaret Lewis, *Ngaio Marsh: A Life* (London: Chatto & Windus, 1991), 68.
3. Lewis, 40. See also Kathryne Slate McDorman, *Ngaio Marsh* (Boston: Twayne Publishers/G. K. Hall & Co., 1991).
4. Lewis, 68.
5. Lewis, x.
6. Ngaio Marsh, Letter to author, 9 July 1979.
7. Ngaio Marsh, Letter to author, 13 November 1979.
8. Alzina Stone Dale and Barbara Sloan Hendershott, *Mystery Readers Walking Guide: London* (Lincolnwood, Il.: Passport Books, 1987), xviii-ix, 189-200.
9. Lewis, 61.

10. Ngaio Marsh, *A Wreath for Rivera,* (also published as *Swing, Brother, Swing*), (New York: Berkley Medallion Books, Berkley Publishing Corporation, 1962), 11.

11. Marsh, *BBHD*, 305-06.

12. Ngaio Marsh, *Light Thickens* (New York: Jove Books, 1983), 230-231.

13. Ngaio Marsh, *A Surfeit of Lampreys* (also published as *Death of a Peer*), (New York: Jove, 1980), 15; cited hereafter as *SL.*

14. *SL*, 20.

15. *SL*, 24.

16. *SL*, 235.

17. Ngaio Marsh, *Death in a White Tie,* (London: Fontana/Collins, 1968), 54-55.

18. Ngaio Marsh, "Roderick Alleyn," in *The Collected Short Fiction of Ngaio Marsh,* ed. Douglas G. Greene, (New York: International Polygonics, Ltd. 1989), 19, 24.

19. Ngaio Marsh, *Black as He's Painted,* (New York: Pyramid Books, 1976), 14-15.

20. Marsh, *BBHD,* 340.

21. Greene, 7.

Roderick Alleyn and the New Professionals

by Kathryne S. McDorman

All forms of fiction are an appropriate and vital source for historians who wish to examine popular attitudes and social changes in a particular era. British detective fiction that reached its apogee in the interwar years of the twentieth century, the so-called "Golden Age," proves to be especially fertile for the cultural historian. Because it is a democratic fiction that appealed to readers in all strata of British society from the modest working man to the dons of Oxford and Cambridge, it reflects many of their concerns. Detective fiction has become the twentieth-century version of the novel of manners. Of the four Grand Dames who wrote classical detective fiction, New Zealand born Ngaio Marsh is in a unique position as the colonial "outsider" among the "insider" authors such as Agatha Christie, Margery Allingham and Dorothy L. Sayers. She brings a special perspective to analyze social change. In her work one senses the rigidity of class distinction and perceives in the character of her protagonist, Roderick Alleyn, a symbol of fundamental transformation in attitudes towards both class and professionalism in modern Britain.

For centuries Britain had relied on loyal amateurs to govern, keep the peace, and make national policy. From the Justices of the Peace to Members of Parliament to the soldiers who won the empire, there was little training or rigorous preparation afforded the men who assumed such responsibilities; indeed, there was almost a hint of vulgarity about the very idea of employing professionals to serve the state. This began to change in the nineteenth century with the institution of a professional Indian Civil Service and Edward Cardwell's and R. B. Haldane's Army Reforms for more professional standards and better organization in the military, yet proceeded slowly in the next century with entrenched class attitudes having to retreat at every advance of professionalism. Ironically, ideas about which, if any, professions were acceptable for the educated upper classes, moved from the fringes of empire back to the mother country instead of being exported from her. It was acceptable for an aristocrat to serve in the military police to keep the peace in India long before it was respectable for that same aristocrat to keep the peace at home. The Metropolitan Police Force was one of the institutions struggling to adopt new ideas, and Marsh's Alleyn would have understood the difficulties.

As a necessary corollary of advancing professionalism the strict stratification of the social classes had to crack. Competitive exams with fixed standards, assessments of performance, with promotion based upon these standards and routine evaluations imply a socially and professionally mobile work force. As two recent films have indicated, the change was slow. In *Chariots of Fire* the Cambridge dons excoriated the youthful Harold Samuels who dared to use a professional trainer to prepare for the Olympic Games. He was reminded that Cambridge men were proud of their amateur standing. *Remains of the Day* has a striking scene set in the 1930's in which an American millionaire warns the British that their well-born amateurs in the Foreign Office are promoting disastrous diplomatic polices. He predicts that family connections and networks of social influence that had traditionally secured and guaranteed place and advancement would pass away quickly.

Marsh lived in an England undergoing these subtle, but radical changes in thinking. With her discerning eye as a New Zealander, she had a more disinterested and therefore clearer view of this phenomenon than her great contemporaries. By comparison, both Sayers and Allingham clung to the formula set by Conan Doyle and others. Dorothy L. Sayers's Peter Wimsey and Margery Allingham's Albert Campion were aristocratic amateur sleuths whose collaborators were their manservants. Only Marsh envisions an aristocratic cop whose right hand man is a working-class inspector struggling to meet the requirements to rise in the ranks of Scotland Yard. Somerset Maugham describes the convention that had dominated the genre until Alleyn appeared:

> The police officer is generally a conventional figure with little individuality; at best he is astute, painstaking and logical; but for the most part he is unimaginative and obtuse. Then of course he serves as a convenient foil to the amateur's brilliance. The amateur may be endowed with a number of distinctive features which give him some semblance of a human being. By discovering things that had escaped the inspector from Scotland Yard he can prove that the amateur is more intelligent and more competent than the professional, and this is naturally satisfying to the readers of a country where the expert is always regarded with suspicion (1).

In order to examine these changes in the context of Marsh's canon, especially in the first decade of Alleyn's existence, it is necessary to identify certain characteristics of a professional and of "professionalism." Fundamentally, a professional is one who identifies with a set of assumptions, a code of ethics or set of purposes that he shares with others of like mind, a sort of "in crowd" phenomenon. There has been some rite of passage in acquiring this identity and there may well be an ambivalence at times about the demands imposed and the constriction of individual expression implicit in being an insider. Usually the rite of passage into a profession involves an initiation into a special kind of expertise or knowledge that sets the expert apart. In successful professionals the identity is so strong that it bleeds across the boundaries of time and space--a doctor is always a doctor, even if out of the hospital or examining room; a lawyer will retain an adversarial point of view away from the courtroom; and a detective cannot resist detecting if presented with a puzzle or crime.

By these standards Alleyn is the quintessential professional. He is called upon and never refuses to investigate a murder whether he is off duty attending a play, on holiday thousands of miles from his own shores, or as in later books, weekending with his wife who is pursuing her profession as a portrait painter. No matter how far from the Yard he strays, the mantle of "police" weighs heavily upon his shoulders and, though careful of local police sensibilities, he readily asserts his authority at the scene of the crime.

It took the British several centuries to be comfortable with the idea of a professional police force. These responsibilities were formerly in the hands of the great landholders who enjoyed the full measure of legal, economic, and social power over their charges. Their prestige had kept

the peace in a rural society with a limited population. That
these responsibilities should be in the hands of those trained
and paid to assume them engendered a fear in the British mind
traceable back to Oliver Cromwell and his thinly disguised
military dictatorship in the mid-seventeenth century. It was
not until the radical transformations and social eruptions of the
Industrial Revolution occurred that English people would
contemplate a police force of any sort.

Eager not to duplicate the French gendarmerie,
nineteenth-century reformers passed the Metropolitan Police
Act in 1829 that established an unarmed force limited to
London. By 1839 the London police were so successful that
other cities in Britain followed suit. The police were readily
identifiable blue uniformed constables known somewhat
pejoratively as "bluebottles" or "bobbies." It took British
society another generation to acknowledge that plainclothes,
less identifiable police could be useful also. The detective
branch was founded in 1842 and the Criminal Investigation
Department in 1878. Problems were immediately apparent:
the two branches chafed against each other because the terms
of advancement from one rank to the other were not clearly
spelled out, and the constables perceived the detectives as
condescending. Their enmity was not easily resolved; pay,
pensions, and promotions were still making headlines and
being hammered out in the force when Ngaio Marsh visited
England in 1928.

What is more important, the police force as a whole
was not certain of its status. Was it regarded as a worthy
profession or not? Sir Robert Peel, the father of the
Metropolitan Police Act, had insisted that he did not
wish to employ gentlemen as Commissioned Officers,
Superintendents, or Inspectors because he was sure they
would be "above their work." Towards the end of the

nineteenth century gentlemen did indeed begin to fill some professions. The redoubtable Oxford University offered training and competitive examinations for the Colonial Service and the Indian and Ceylon police forces. The police force at home benefited from this same enthusiasm. As David Ascoli maintains, "The old order had changed and out of the smoke of battle had emerged, however surprisingly, a new kind of professionalism" (2). In 1890 New Scotland Yard moved into its newly designed headquarters described as a Baronial Hall. T. A. Critchley notes that the move into a new location denoted "a spirit of change that was converting a job into a vocation" (3).

The new professionalism and new, more dignified quarters were accompanied by technical developments in crime detection. The use of fingerprints was accepted by 1900, and by 1902 they were regarded as "corroborative evidence." Also in 1902 a training school for detectives had been established at New Scotland Yard and then expanded into the Police Training School at Peel House in Westminster. Despite these advances, the public continued to dine on scurrilous rumors of police corruption and allegations that their careless or dishonest work resulted in wrongful convictions of innocent persons.

By the end of World War I the force was once again in need of revitalization. It had suffered the loss of some of its most talented personnel who had joined the army and, like so many young men, had been slaughtered in the fields of Flanders. Those who remained behind shocked the public when, at a critical point in the war, they struck for higher wages. Though the Prime Minister, David Lloyd-George, averted a genuine disruption of public order at that particular moment, he pledged that after the war a careful study and reform of the police force would be carried out.

In 1919 a Parliamentary committee under Lord Desborough proposed legislation to improve conditions and recognized that many of the complaints of the police were indeed legitimate. The Desborough Report demanded a healthy police force as the only way of insuring good public order, and recommended elevating the constables whom they recognized as "semi-professional men." The economic woes of the 1920's prevented Desborough's work from having any immediate results in improving real wages; consequently, morale was at low ebb in 1928 and 1929. The newspapers screamed out ugly headlines about scandals of police on the take, thereby savaging the integrity of the force. This was the England, the London, that Ngaio Marsh first visited with all the breathless enthusiasm of a novitiate. Six years later, she would create the most thoroughly admirable and the only professional policeman among the Grand Dames of Golden Age detective fiction.

Roderick Alleyn could have joined the force in the 1920's under the reforming administration of Police Commissioner Byng, who was appointed in 1928 and pledged to "re-inspire" the disillusioned force, restore its professional pride, and recreate the measure of public confidence that it had enjoyed after the General Strike of 1926. His task was not easy, in part because the force had been slow to accept the social revolution of the twentieth century. In spite of the Desborough Committee and the increasing sophistication of police methods world wide, Britain's New Scotland Yard had remained an "ultra-conservative artisan institution, still wedded to a hierarchical structure...and, with its lack of incentives still attracted brawn rather than brains" (4).

Ngaio Marsh remained vague about Alleyn's motivation for choosing police work. Surely the Foreign Office that he had quitted for the police offered a more

socially acceptable career. Indeed the Foreign Office was
famous for its younger sons of aristocrats, like Alleyn, who
proudly conducted their business during "gentleman's hours"
and by amateur standards. His mother, Lady Alleyn, muses,
"I always feel, darling, that you should not have left the
Foreign Office, but at the same time, I am a great believer in
everybody doing what he wants to, and I do enjoy hearing
about your cases" (5). Lady Carrados, another socialite,
remarks of Lady Alleyn's two sons, "One is a deadly baronet
and the other is a detective." She admits that Chief Inspector
Alleyn has grown famous by his successes and evaluates him
as, "Terribly good looking and remote. He was in the Foreign
Office when the war broke out and then after the war he
suddenly became a detective. I can't tell you why. Not that it
matters" (6). Both of these society ladies are being rather
artificially tolerant. Also in *Artists in Crime* Virginia Van
Maes, a social climbing American, remarks, "Gee Mr. Alleyn,
I never knew that your detective force was recruited from
your aristocracy" (7). Despite her gaucheries Miss Van Maes
was correct in her naive observation. It was not uncommon
for the younger brothers of baronets to seek a profession, but
for a high society gentleman to become a professional
policeman was distinctly eccentric in the 1920's and 1930's.

Alleyn exhibits some marks of his privileged status:
his Oxford degree, a quotable knowledge of Shakespeare, and
his fastidiousness. In the novel in which he is introduced, *A
Man Lay Dead*, Marsh allows young socialite Angela North
to describe him:

>   Alleyn did not resemble a plain-clothes police-
>   man she felt sure, nor was he in the romantic
>   manner--white faced and gimlet eyed. He looked
>   like one of her Uncle Hubert's friends, the sort

who would 'do' for house parties. He was
tall and lean, his hair was dark, and his eyes
gray with corners that turned down. They
looked like he would smile easily, but his
mouth didn't (8).

Angela also notices that his hands and his mellifluous
voice indicate a grand gentleman. Her fiancé Nigel Bathgate,
Alleyn's Watson in the early novels, describes him as an
"athletic don with a bit of army somewhere. No, that's not
right; it's too commonplace. He's faunish. And yet he's got all
the right things for 'teckery" (9). No one is quite certain how
a policeman should look, but all agree that whatever that look
is, Alleyn doesn't have it.

In the course of his investigations, his pedigree and his
to-the-manor-born manner impress some and offend others.
In *Death in a White Tie* Alleyn's social standing enables him
to penetrate easily the closed drawing rooms and extract his
murderer. On being interviewed, a vital witness, Mrs. Halcut-
Hackett gushes, "I never realized that I was speaking to Lady
Alleyn's famous son" (10). Rapt in her admiration, she forgets
her frigidity and delivers important clues. Inwardly he writhes
"under the blatant recognition of his snob value" (11).

For each of those who curry favor with the prominent
detective there are at least a dozen who freeze, snarl, or
remain sullen because of his elegant ways. In every novel
someone, usually a suspect, is bound to reveal distrust or
disgust:

"What sort of breed are you?" asked Mr. Saint.
"Gentleman 'tec or comedian of the Yard, or
what?"

"My dear Mr. Saint you make me feel quite
shy."

"Ow yow yow yow," Saint echoed the
inspector's pleasant voice with the exasper-
ated facetiousness of a street urchin. "All
Oxford and Cambridge and hot air," he added
savagely.

"Only Oxford and that's nothing nowadays"
(12).

Another suspect, Captain Withers, recoils at Alleyn's questions
and snarls, "You seem to be a gentleman. One of the new
breed at the Yard, aren't you?" (13). Both the upper and
lower classes sense a real incongruity between Alleyn's social
standing, education, and his profession as a policeman.

In exploring the incongruity between the "new" breed
of police and their artisan image, Marsh reflects a deep
division in public opinion over the status of police officers,
both of the CID. and the uniformed branch. Many
commissioners sought to improve the police "image" only to
be frustrated by suspicion within the force itself and from
social egalitarians outside it. In 1930, Police Commissioner
Dixon proposed the National Police College through which
would pass all those who sought promotion in the ranks. The
Police Federation, a union-like organization, successfully
resisted this change, but when Lord Trenchard became Police
Commissioner after Dixon's resignation, he created seismic
disturbances in the force. It was Trenchard who created
Roderick Alleyn's rank, Chief Inspector, and who unabashedly
sought to recruit Alleyn's caliber of men into the force. In
1932 he created the Metropolitan Police College at Hendon,

into which men could be admitted through two pathways: by competitive examination and special recommendation, or directly from colleges and universities.

Though some interpreted this as creating a meritocracy, others like Labour Member Aneurin Bevan in the House of Commons snapped, "It is an entirely fascist development...to make the police force more amenable to the orders of the Carlton Club and Downing Street" (14). Ngaio Marsh echoes this conflict from the mouth of her cynical Bolshevik Nurse Banks in *The Nursing Home Murder* as she scoffs at Alleyn, "I know your type--the gentleman police-man--the latest development of the capitalist system. You've got where you are by influence while better men do bigger work for a slave's pittance" (15). *The Police Review* also bemoaned the creation of the college, "It is 'class' legislation with a vengeance. In practice the plan will mean that the higher ranks of the Force will be filled in the main by young men who enter the college directly from public school and university" (16). Despite the objections, Hendon opened in 1934, and though it closed in the war years, it did help to improve the quality of police training and to enhance the status of the force as a profession. Finally the English demanded that qualifications and professional standards for their own police force be on a par with the police whom they trained to keep order in the dependent empire.

Marsh does not reveal Alleyn's professional training other than through memories he shares with Fox about the long hours he remembers walking a beat and memorizing the *Police Code and Procedure*. Once he is asked,

"Have you been through the Police College?"

"Not precisely, Madam."

"Indeed?" said Miss Wade, squinting
curiously at him, "but you speak nicely."

"You are kind."

"A superior school perhaps? The
advantages---"

"My parents gave me all the advantages they
could afford," agreed Alleyn solemnly" (17).

According to Earnestine Wade, who is the oldest character in
this novel, Alleyn's manners and speech would indicate that he
was an educated gentleman, but as for her and for so many
other characters, his profession confused her perception of
him.
    Marsh reveals the why and how Alleyn became a
policeman in a mysterious Victorian stage whisper behind her
hand, but she explores forthrightly how he views his
profession.   In these first books of the canon, Marsh
introduces him as facetious, foppish, and apparently casual
about his job; in later books she transforms him into a sensitive
and loyal friend and a loving husband. In his first incarnation
in *A Man Lay Dead*, Alleyn is almost unbearably fatuous.
Asked why he is agitated, he responds, "You've guessed my
boyish secret. I've been given a murder to solve--aren't I a
lucky little detective?" (18). In *Enter a Murderer*, his second
appearance, he trills, "Am I tidy?...It looks bad not to be tidy
for an arrest" (19). Beneath this affectedness, however, is a
man of heightened sensitivity who, while ruthlessly determined
to ferret out the murderer, knows that revelations that are
bound to surface in a murder investigation can cause pain to
the innocent and guilty alike. He is the "filthy crime dentist,"

as he calls himself, who probes until he causes pain and hauls in someone "wriggling like a nerve on the end of a wire" (20). Because he is the extractor of wrongdoing and malice he is isolated from his fellow humans. When he has to arrest an old school chum of Nigel Bathgate, he is almost apologetic: "Well, Bathgate...never make friends with a policeman" (21). By the time of *The Nursing Home Murder* and *Death in Ecstasy*, he has begun to describe himself as a "wheel of the machine" of justice that is a "'complicated and automatic machinery...[which] once started...cannot [be] switched off" (22). Later he explains, "I receive facts...as a spider does flies" (23). For all of his mechanistic and predatory imagery Alleyn still shudders at the look of apprehension that passes across the face of an innocent witness, and at the end of *The Nursing Home Murder* he sighs that he doesn't see many happy endings on the Force--confirming that he is not exactly the stuff of which cold and hardened police are made.

By the publication of *Vintage Murder* Alleyn has developed a case of disillusionment and depression. Having traveled to New Zealand in order to restore his spirits and soothe his bruised nerves, he finds himself once again present at a murder and is asked to assist the local police in solving the crime. Though he feels initial dismay, he agrees to help in the investigation. Writing to Fox back in London to ask him to check a lead, he admits, "I confess I am surprised at myself and can only suppose that I must like 'teckery--an amazing discovery" (24). By the time of *Artists in Crime* he is back in his professional role in London.

> The Scotland Yard officials had arrived, and
> with their appearance the case, for the first time,
> seemed to take on a familiar complexion. The
> year he had spent away from England clicked

back into the past on the sight of those familiar
overcoated and bowler-hatted figures with their
cases and photographic impedimenta (25).

Both Alleyn and his associates, especially Mr. Fox, relish the
homecoming. In the course of this dual murder novel, Alleyn
falls in love with Agatha Troy, the famous artist. A murder
investigation is scarcely an ideal environment in which to
plight one's troth; he squirms miserably in front of Troy, the
one person he wants most to impress, betraying at every turn
his deep ambivalence about his work. After suffering what he
regards as her displays of "frigid courtesy" during which he
imagines that she "resented the very sight of him and
everything he stood for," he reluctantly confesses his love for
her. When she does not immediately reciprocate his feelings,
he muses, "I think if we had met again in a different way, you
might have loved me" (26).

His assumptions about her revulsion toward his
profession prove only partially correct. He grows morbidly
self-deprecating during his next meeting with her in *Death in
à White Tie* almost whining:

> If you painted a surrealist picture of me I
> would be made of Metropolitan Police Note-
> books, one eye would be set in a keyhole, my
> hands would be occupied with somebody else's
> private correspondence. The background
> would be a morgue and the whole pretty con-
> ceit wreathed with festoons of blue tape and
> hangman's rope (27).

Fortunately by the end of the novel Troy confesses her love
for him, allowing such painful ruminations and self pitying to

cease. In subsequent novels he will occasionally mutter about his profession getting in the way of his life and his family. Troy is never easy with his choice of profession, but she comes to rely upon his protective strength and his profound commitment to her. Whatever aura of disapproval might cling to his police work, his wife and his friends succeed in ignoring it. Alleyn's elevated social status underlines the profound class consciousness in Scotland Yard itself. Distinctions of status and wages abraded relations between the detectives of the CID. and the uniformed constables. The former earned salaries and were accorded some respect; the latter earned hourly wages and were sometimes the target of ribald humor construing them as thick headed. Too often this image was reinforced by detectives who deprecated those below them. In the early books Alleyn, though not rude, refers to his uniformed associates as "bluebottles," a not altogether kindly slang term, and breezily dismisses their efforts. In the later *Death in a White Tie* he has learned to appreciate their worth,

> ...the hunt is up...Have you ever read in the
> crime books about the relentless detective
> who swears he'll get his man if it takes him the
> rest of his life? That's me, Troy, and I always
> thought it rather a bogus idea. It is bogus in a
> way, too. The real heroes of criminal investi-
> gation are Detective Constables X, Y and Z--
> the men who follow up all the dreary threads
> of routine without any personal feeling or inter-
> est, who swear no full round oaths, but who
> nevertheless, do get their man in the end; with
> a bit of luck and the infinite capacity for taking
> pains (28).

This outburst is the most emotionally charged and positive view of police work in the canon. Despite Allen's passion, the murderer in this book is uncovered by the very routine and exacting procedures typical of the ultimate professional.

Nowhere is Alleyn's transformation from facetious gadfly or neurotic suitor to thoughtful professional detective more apparent than in his attitudes towards his assistant, Edward Fox. Though Eric Routley calls Fox "Alleyn's right hand man: unambitious, contented, efficient and marvelously communicated from the very first" (29), the relationship between them was far from secure in Marsh's early novels. In the first three, Alleyn was far more attached to young Nigel Bathgate, a man from his own social class. Fox is only incidental in *A Man Lay Dead*, and in *Enter a Murderer* Alleyn is ill at ease with his stolid associate. Exhibiting his most affected and sardonic style, he scores off Fox to show off to Bathgate:

> "Fox, my valued old one...wing your way
> down to Miss Vaughn's dressing room and get
> the foot of my grandmother's hare which you
> will find on the dressing table. Fetch me that
> foot and be thou here again 'ere Leviathan can
> swim a league." Inspector Fox cast his eyes
> heavenward and did as he was bid... (30).

Later when Alleyn reflects that he feels like Hamlet after he killed Polonius, Fox answers humbly, "Shakespeare...I don't read that sort of thing myself" (31). By *Death in Ecstasy* Fox has gained more confidence around his chief when he engages in a flight of verbal fancy: "'Come off it, Sir' said Fox with a grin" (32). In the same novel Alleyn invites Fox's collaboration, "Light your pipe my Foxkin, and let's do a bit of 'teckery" (33). Alleyn even reveals some of his depression about their work referring to it as "degrading" and musing that "Custom makes monsters of us all." Asking Fox if he feels the same way, Alleyn answers his own question, "No, I don't think you do. You are too nice-minded. You are always quite sane. And such a wise old bird, too." Fox responds gently to his now beloved boss,

> ...I know how you feel about homicide cases.
> I'd put it down to your imagination. You're a
> a very imaginative man, I'd say. I'm not at all
> fanciful myself, but it does seem queer to me
> sometimes, how calm-like we get to work,
> grousing about the routine, put out because
> our meals don't come regular, and all the time
> there's a trap and a rope and a broken neck at
> the end if we do our job properly. Well there
> it is. It's got to be done (34).

In *The Nursing Home Murder*, published the same year as *Death in Ecstasy*, Marsh has consigned Nigel Bathgate to the periphery and has elevated the unassuming Inspector Fox to Watson status. The mystery revolves around prominent socialite Cicely O'Callaghan, who requests that Scotland Yard investigate the death of her husband. Fox is the first to see her, but she quickly makes it clear that she prefers to confide in his boss. Fox replies, "Yes, he is rather well known. He's a very highly educated man. Quite a different type from me, you might say" (35). Mrs. O'Callaghan might indeed say that, but by now Alleyn would not. For his humility and complete lack of rancor and jealousy, Fox deserved better than the brusque superiority with which Alleyn had treated him previously and with which the O'Callaghans of the world still did. It is Fox who becomes the professional anchor for the fey Roderick Alleyn, as Troy becomes his personal one. Marsh creates a bond between the two men that suggests a healing between the ranks on the police force. It is the breaking down of the social barriers and the recognition that all the ranks share an equal commitment to professionalism. The Alleyn-Fox alliance suggests that all the best qualities of every member of the Force can be utilized. Both Alleyn's finely educated mind and social skills as well as Fox's steady working-class conservatism offer Britain and her police the best gifts for surviving the chaotic forces of the twentieth century.

Ngaio Marsh's creation of Roderick Alleyn marks a new kind of hero in detective fiction. Heretofore the professional police force had been conventionally portrayed by writers as ignorant, lower-class men not clever enough to solve a crime without the assistance of the bright, witty gentleman amateur. Looking back at Dickens and Trollope and at Marsh's great contemporaries, Sayers and Allingham, one realizes the convention had a long and rich tradition. Michael Innes (a.k.a. J. I. M. Stewart) comments that it becomes increasingly less convincing in the modern world.

> ...there has been an increasing problem of
> verisimilitude here during the later phases in
> the development of the detective story. The
> average reader will not be wholly uninformed
> about modern criminal investigation as a highly
> developed and sophisticated machine whose
> operatives can call upon a number of scientific
> disciplines. The spectacle of so powerful an
> engine ticking over idly while the Great

Detective's little grey cells go to work is one
hard to render convincing (36).

It is Marsh who brings detective fiction into greater
harmony with the vicissitudes of twentieth-century life by
creating a clever, well born, professional policeman. Of
course her professional policeman is ambivalent; he is breaking
the rules and challenging the long held mythology that Britain
is a nation run by dedicated amateurs. He knows that he is
serving justice by solving murders, but he never quite escapes
the uneasy shame of his professional status. Like others of his
social class, Alleyn has not quite adapted to the end of
aristocratic political domination symbolized by the 1911
Parliament Act and the impact of World War I that ended
Britain's worldwide hegemony. Alleyn is symbolic of the
social and professional revolution coursing through the
interwar years.

By creating Alleyn's character as an Oxford educated
policeman, Marsh clears the way for Adam Dalgliesh, Henry
Tibbett, and Inspector Wexford, and promotes the ideal of
professionalism so reluctantly accepted in British society in
modern times. More than any other Grand Dame author she
transcends the formulaic detective story genre. Her books
should be counted among the novels of manners for their
social commentary. Novels of manners, whether they are
detective stories or not, mirror the conventions of their time
and how changes in attitudes affect and transform those
conventions.

ENDNOTES

1. William Somerset Maugham, *The Vagrant Mood*
   (Garden City, New York: Doubleday and Co., Inc.,
   1953), 115.
2. David Ascoli, *The Queen's Peace: The Origins and
   Development of the Metropolitan Police 1829-1979*
   (London: Hamish Hamilton, 1979), 165.
3. T. A. Critchley, *A History of Police in England and
   Wales* (London: Constable, 1978), 171.
4. Ascoli, 222.
5. Ngaio Marsh, *Artists in Crime* (New York: Jove
   Books, 1980), 17; hereafter cited in the text as *AC*.
6. Ngaio Marsh, *Death in a White Tie* (New York: Jove
   Books, 1977), 18; hereafter cited in the text as *DWT*.
7. Marsh, *AC*, 16.
8. Ngaio Marsh, *A Man Lay Dead* (New York: Sheridan
   House, 1942), 67; hereafter cited in the text as *MLD*.
9. Ngaio Marsh, *Death in Ecstasy* (London: Geoffrey
   Bles, 1936), 153; hereafter cited in the text as *DE*.
10. Marsh, *DWT*, 225.
11. Marsh, *DWT*, 225-26.
12. Ngaio Marsh, *Enter a Murderer* (London: Fontana
    Collins, 1964), 51; hereafter cited in the text as *EM*.
13. Marsh, *DWT*, 128.
14. As quoted by Ascoli, 234.
15. Ngaio Marsh, *The Nursing Home Murder* (London:
    Geoffrey Bles, 1935), 123; hereafter cited in the text as
    NHM.
16. *The Police Review*, May 19, 1933, n.p.
17. Marsh, *DE*, 108.
18. Marsh, *MLD*, 60.
19. Marsh, *EM*, 145.

20. Marsh, *DWT*, 112.
21. Marsh, *EM*, 183.
22. Marsh, *NHM*, 237.
23. Marsh, *DE*, 56.
24. Ngaio Marsh, *Vintage Murder* (London: Geoffrey Bles, 1937), 173; hereafter cited in the text as *VM*.
25. Marsh, *AC*, 44.
26. Marsh, *AC*, 245.
27. Marsh, *DWT*, 245.
28. Marsh, *DWT*, 97.
29. Eric Routley, *The Puritan Pleasures of the Detective Story: A Personal Monograph* (London: Gollancz, 1972), 147.
30. Marsh, *EM*, 63.
31. Marsh, *EM*, 169.
32. Marsh, *DE*, 233.
33. Marsh, *DE*, 132.
34. Marsh, *DE*, 234-35.
35. Marsh, *NHM*, 58.
36. Michael Innes, "Introduction," in Edmund Crispin's *Swan Song* (New York: Avon Books, 1980), 8.

The Mannered Mystery: *Death of a Peer*

by B. A. Pike

Death of a Peer is the eleventh of Ngaio Marsh's novels, first published by Little, Brown in 1940. In January, 1941, Collins Crime Club issued the first British edition, with the variant title *Surfeit of Lampreys*. Since few things wear as well as good detective fiction, it continues in print to this day, still asserting after fifty years its claim on the discriminating reader in sympathy with its aims and achievements. Like all the best detective novels, its primary concern is to intrigue and amuse a sophisticated audience. It is not for those who feel threatened by "elitism," nor for those who dismiss the cerebral detective story as merely a matter of formula. There are no car chases and the bedroom scenes simply advance the action.

The novel is characteristic of its author, scrupulous in contrivance and buoyant in narrative, with much theatrical bravura and touches of macabre intensity. The action embraces the farce of a ludicrous charade and an ambitious scene of pure Grand Guignol. The exposition is leisurely and seventy pages have passed before "a thin blade of sound, sharp and insistent" (1), heralds a new and quickening phase of the narrative; but once the action proper is launched, there is never a dull moment.

The eponymous Lampreys are a feckless, uppercrust family who survive by virtue of their position and a well-tried capacity for bailing out: "Something always happens to save

143

them. They know they will land on their feet" (2). They are compared to the Micawbers, but are perhaps even closer to Harold Skimpole, whose airy attitude to money and debt and bailiffs precisely prefigures their own. They are "museum pieces. Carryovers from another age," still "behaving in the grand leisured manner without the necessary backing" (3).

There are eight Lampreys: typically, Lord and Lady Charles have seen no reason to limit the size of their family. Lord Charles is the sole surviving brother of the Marquis of Wutherwood and succeeds to the title when the latter is murdered. The "sharp...insistent" scream is his widow's reaction to her discovery of his fatally wounded state.

The Lampreys dominate the novel and any discussion of it must largely be a discussion of them. The tension between what they say and do and the devotion they inspire in others adds considerably to the interest of the narrative. Three people pay fervent tribute to the special quality that sets them apart: Roberta Grey, their young New Zealand friend; Dr. Kantripp, their family doctor; and Nigel Bathgate, familiar from earlier novels as Roderick Alleyn's Boswell-cum-Watson. There is some excuse for Roberta, since the Lampreys caught her young, but the doctor and Nigel are old enough to know better; they are experienced, worldly men, whose attempts to persuade Alleyn that the family is above suspicion make them appear foolish. It is a measure of Dame Ngaio's skill that she enables us to see both how the Lampreys have acquired their reputation and how little in some ways they have deserved it.

Their popularity leans heavily on their much-vaunted "charm," a nebulous quality that all but eludes Dr. Kantripp when Alleyn challenges him to define it. Nigel does no better, and it is left to Roberta to state a fundamental truth that goes some way to explaining the Lampreys' behavior. She is "visited by the odd idea" that, in the years since their last meeting, she has grown older but "the young Lampreys had merely grown taller;" and she concludes that "they are like children" and only seem to be "grown-up" (4).

Roberta's perception has much to commend it, since the evidence to support it is abundant and inescapable. Like children, the Lampreys are self-absorbed and lacking in purpose, yielding to impulse, and living for the moment. They play extrovert games and make fun of their elders; and they leave money to take care of itself, with no thought of having to earn it.

All six adult Lampreys have the Skimpole attitude to money and they none of them allow its absence to interfere with their routines and pleasures. They follow to the limit Lady Charles's dictum of not jumping a financial fence until one meets it, leaving creditors to take their chance of being paid and accepting bailiffs as a necessary evil. They live in two adjacent flats near Cadogan Square with a butler, a nanny, a cook, and two maids. Though they have run out of money, they invite Roberta for an extended stay, heedless of the additional drain on their resources. Somehow they contrive for her a "a dazzling evening" at a theatre and a nightclub; somehow they manage to acquire a rare and expensive sherry as a blandishment for Lord Wutherwood. Henry knows which restaurant will let him "chalk it up"; and his mother laments in retrospect the "mad moment" in which her husband actually paid for a valuable Chinese pot.

None of the older children has a job, though Henry and his younger brothers, the twins Stephen and Colin, are all in their twenties. Frid Lamprey attends drama classes in the vague hope of making her way in the theatre. Lady Charles deplores the fact that her husband "doesn't happen to have a head for sums" (5); but her own idea of economy is to stop taking *Punch* and *The Tatler* and to dispense with table napkins. Lord Charles is at least aware of the need to provide for his brood, but his schemes are ill-conceived and invariably fail. In his brother's scathing words, he even makes a failure of "the noble art of sponging" (6).

To persuade Lord Wutherwood to bail them out, they plan to offer him his favorite sherry and give him the pot that was actually paid for. They also decide to perform a charade to "make him feel gay." Roberta's attempt to point out the absurdity of all this is overruled by "the mad logic of their scheming" (7). Lord Wutherwood's reaction is predictably dismissive: he ignores the charade and refuses to help, enraging all the Lampreys except Lady Charles and her youngest son, Michael, who are not in the front line.

The younger Lampreys react like naughty children to the failure of their charade, turning "white" or "scarlet with fury" according to complexion. They disregard Michael's anxiety at having lost track of the pot he is to present to his uncle; only Roberta responds to his implicit appeal for help. Later, they eavesdrop on their father's interview with his brother, lying "close together on the floor with their heads to the wall," listening at the crack of a "boarded-up door" (8). Just so might one imagine Five Getting into Trouble in something by Enid Blyton.

The vaunted kindness of the Lampreys is absent on a number of occasions, not just when Michael is left to fend for himself. Frid makes clear her intention to foist onto her younger siblings the chore of escorting Roberta to the sights of London. Stephen comments callously on Lady Wutherwood's hysteria at the sight of her dying husband. Since he shared her experience, it is forgivable that he should feel "sick," but he has no right to call her "disgraceful." Lady Charles is dismissive of her brother-in-law's interest in drainage, making it appear ridiculous, without clearly having any way of knowing whether it was or not. She and Frid separately sneer at Lord Wutherwood's collection of Chinese procelain, but Alleyn recalls a "loan exhibition" of his treasures, so demonstrating how their view is limited by prejudice and ignorance. Most deplorably, both Lady Charles and Frid argue that, since she is likely to be "locked up" anyway, Lady Wutherwood might as well take the blame for the murder, even if she did not commit it (9).

Lord Charles accuses his brother of being "a hell of a snob" but without supplying chapter and verse to support the charge. Indeed, the plan to exploit Lord Wutherwood's supposed snobbery founders when he shows no inclination to "crawl with horror at the publicity" of a bankrupt brother but, on the contrary, seems to exult at the prospect (10). Evidence of snobbish traits among the Lampreys does exist, however: in Henry's claim to "hate the poor;" in Frid's assessment of a gift to her mother as "common;" in Stephen's dismissal of his uncle's bowler as "a poisonous hat" that looks "as if it belonged to a bum" (11); in Colin's expressed preference for being "grilled by a gent;" and in a succession of edged remarks from Lady Charles, who describes Nanny Burnaby's gloves as "frightful," refers to her husband's late partner as "a rather nice second-rate little man" (12), and dubs a modest car acquired as an economy measure "that common little horror."

Every instance of charm has it counterweight of vanity, self-interest, insensitivity or snobbish condescension; and it becomes impossible for the reader to endorse Dr. Kantripp's and Nigel's view of the Lampreys. Of course, we know them better than they do: we witness their spats and squabbles and overhear their less endearing remarks. They are good at presenting themselves and know how to charm and amuse. Their social skills are highly developed: they never fail, in Roberta's words, to "rise to situations." Even the murder does not throw them into total disarray. Their conversation may be "preposterous," their schemes no less so, but the Lampreys are "nobody's fools." Though Alleyn calls them "that collection of certifiable grotesques" and they themselves show "great industry in underlining their eccentricity," he concedes that they are "only mad nor'-nor'-west" and can "tell a hawk from a handsaw" (13). Nigel fears that they may have "behaved like lunatics" but Alleyn is able to reassure him that, on the contrary, they have "displayed surprising virtuosity." He is alive to their power to distort and disturb and confides to Fox his fears that "They'll diddle us if we don't look out" (14). He acknowledges the need to tread carefully: "Let us but once lose our tempers with the Lampreys and we are done" (15). They are like "handfuls of wet sand which, as fast as he grasped them, were dragged through his fingers by the action of some mysterious undertow" (16).

They are, nonetheless, undermined continually: by Lord Wutherwood, Inspector Fox, P. C. Martin, even Roberta and, especially, Alleyn. We are not invited to like Lord Wutherwood but we are free, as readers, to assess his judgments dispassionately. They are, by and large, irresistible: the family ought to live more modestly; Lord Charles and his sons should be working; Frid might well be running the household. Lord Charles's defense of his children is eloquent and rather touching, but his brother's rejoinders are unanswerable, especially when he raises the question of "lovin'-kindness" to creditors. Inspector Fox, sedate and imperturbable as ever, contrives to disconcert Lord Charles in their preliminary interview, provoking an outraged "Do you, by God?" (17) by revealing that he already knows of Lord Wutherwood's childless state. He also touches slyly on the uncertainty as to which twin accompanied his uncle and aunt in the lift where Lord Wutherwood was stabbed, "as if the confusion of one's children's identities was the most natural thing in the world" (18). P. C. Martin is subjected to some embarrassment by the Lampreys, who talk in French to forestall his keeping an accurate record of their conversation. Since he speaks French fluently, the situation has a certain piquancy. One welcomes his assessment of their performance as "quite good," merely, and could have wished them, *en masse*, to overhear his judgment.

One of Roberta's functions is to allow Henry to voice occasional doubts about his family and their way of life. He responds to what he calls her "Jane Eyreishness" and recognizes that she "must criticize a little": as, indeed, she does, berating him for feebleness and affectation and expressing wonder that his family do not find "shaming" their inability to pay their way. During the murder investigation, her presence is a constant reminder that the standard decencies do largely obtain. The distance between her and the Lampreys is emphasized by her extreme reaction to a comment by Alleyn on the eavesdropping in which she has hesitantly joined: she is overcome with humiliation, her "cheeks...burning coals," in "a nightmare of shame." Henry, reminded of the same occasion, merely remarks, "One up to you, sir" (19). Alleyn himself is, of course, the principal scourge of the Lampreys, as well as a yardstick against which they may be measured. He is, as always, the *chevalier sans peur et sans reproche*, a man of absolute integrity, punctilious and courteous, compact of all the virtues: modest, clear-eyed, humorous, sensitive, imaginative. It is small wonder that, in comparison, the Lampreys' shams and subterfuges appear so "second-rate," to borrow a word from Lady Charles. He does not trust them and, with the exception of young Michael, sees no reason to think well of them. Unlike Dame Ngaio herself, he never lets them off the hook.

He proceeds by stealth, more discomposing than directly damaging. He interviews them all, except Frid, who could hardly be more effectively quashed, since she professes herself agog to encounter "Handsome Alleyn" in the flesh. His comments about her are unambiguous: she is "That devilish girl" and is "as hard as they come." She is one of the objects of his remarks on the self-absorption of "Young people of both sexes between the ages of sixteen and twenty-six" (20). Her elder brothers are, of course, the others. He affects the breathing of both Lord and Lady Charles, rendering the former breathless and causing the latter to "draw in her breath." He persuades Patch, the younger daughter, to overcome "the liveliest reluctance" and come clean about the eavesdropping via carpet and boarded-up door. When the twins rejoin their family, he has "turned them inside out and hung them up to dry" (21). He unnerves Henry repeatedly, to the point where he turns "on his heel" and escapes "blindly into the flat" or is "disconcerted" and "startled," with "an overtone of helplessness" in his voice (22). Even their champions come ill out of their encounters with Alleyn: Roberta over-reacting to her guilt about the eavesdropping and lying to save her friends; Nigel made continually to appear a sentimental, dimwitted nuisance; and Dr. Kantripp driven to a nasty retreat by satire and skepticism. At the end, Alleyn refuses to predict the Lampreys' future courses, reminding Nigel that they are his friends: "God forbid that I should prophesy about them" (23).

The force of the adjectives massed against the Lampreys is considerable: feeble, dishonest, mad, scatter-brained, unstable, reprehensible, preposterous, vague, irresponsible, lazy, unscrupulous, hopeless. Among so much that is negative a few redeeming features declare themselves, something beyond the charm and gaiety and indolent good nature that make them so popular. Their invitation to Roberta, feckless though it is, is generous and truly affectionate. They have established an annuity for Nanny Burnaby that appears inviolate from financial crises. There can be no doubt of the strength of their family feeling, especially as it emerges in the parental anxieties of Lord and Lady Charles. His defense of his children, though it is quickly shot down in flames by Lord Wutherwood, is touchingly heartfelt; and she shows genuine emotion only when one of her children is under threat: her fears for Stephen make her speak in a "voice quite unlike her own." There is also a singular charm in Lord Charles's making "the same movement each night after dinner, always reaching the door before his sons and holding it open with a little bow to his wife as she passed him" (24).

Even so gentle a ritual contributes to the impression of style and panache that emanates from the Lampreys. Though Alleyn is unconvinced by Nigel's contention that "they're beginning to look at this business as a sort of macabre parlour game, with themselves on one side and you on the other" (25), the image of a game is undeniably appropriate to much that they say and do. They are in themselves, effectively, an extended metaphor of performance, enhancing by their activities and attitude the aura of unreality that prevails in the novel. They are isolated from the mundane world both by standard patrician privilege and by their specific refusal to allow it to impinge on them. They are continually acting, either with serious intent, as in their encounters during the murder investigation, or frivolously, as in their tendency to present and dramatize themselves at all times. They love charades and discuss potential themes for them "with passionate enthusiasm." To welcome Roberta, newly arrived from New Zealand, Henry and Frid perform a war-dance on the quayside and assume false noses and beards to enliven the moment of meeting. During the night on the town, Colin has "played the fool, pretended he was a Russian and spoken broken English" (26); and on their return to the flat he, Frid, and Stephen circle like witches, intoning the obvious lines from *Macbeth*.

Frid appears incapable of behaving naturally: her attitude is normally "faintly histrionic" and often more emphatically so. Henry claims that she no longer walks but "sort of paws the ground": "When she comes into the room, she shuts the door behind her and leans against it" (27). Returning from the night club, she adopts "a tragic attitude" before launching into *Macbeth*. When Fox talks informally to the family, she sits in "an attitude of such rapt attention" that Allyn, entering upon the scene, is immediately reminded of her dramatic training. She turns on him "a gaze of embarrassing brilliance," evidently of the kind that projects across footlights. Her "crisp and modish" stance in relation to the murder investigation irritates even her father and Henry, both of whom tell her to be less abrasive. Henry accuses her of projecting her interview with Alleyn as "a fat dramatic scene," ending in his "throwing up the case" because she is "*trop troublante*" (28). She sees her uncle's murder as "a lovely scoop" for Nigel and suggests they invite him to call. A rare touch of genuine feeling escapes her when Lord Wutherwood dismisses her performance in the charade as "Showin' her legs and droopin' about...like a dyin' duck in a thunderstorm" (29). She overhears the judgment and goes "rigid with hatred;" this is hitting her where it hurts.

Stephen and Colin extend the theatrical metaphor in a particularly striking way. Effectively, Colin usurps his twin's identity when he claims to have worked the lift for his dying uncle and distraught aunt. It is clear that this arises from a staple of their relationship: they have had such an "arrangement" since boyhood, each coming to the other's rescue when the need has arisen. Roberta remembers "the forbidden big car" which both claimed to have driven "through a water-race into a bank;" and Henry outlines a fanciful scheme whereby they would "turn crooks" and alibi each other.   Alleyn's interview with Lady Charles is also relevant here. She is evidently acting from the outset and, afterwards, boasts of having achieved her ends: "He hasn't the faintest inkling of what I was up to" (30). Effectively, she parodies herself, rattling on in a "rapid flow of narrative," gay and amusing in what is no doubt her habitual manner; but Alleyn feels "certain that there was more than a touch of bravura" in her performance. It is all "a little too bright, the inconsequence...overstressed, the rhythm somewhere at fault." He considers that what he is seeing is "a perilous imitation of the normal Lady Charles Lamprey by a Lady Charles Lamprey who was by no means normal" (31). As her voice goes "rattling on," he knows she is "trying to force an impression on him"; and though the interview encompasses an emotional outburst from her and his own capitulation to laughter, this emerges as its essential truth.

The Lampreys' detachment from the real world is further developed through Roberta, who is always conscious of being different from them, even when they are at their most warm and enclosing. She becomes aware that, "since the appearance of Alleyn and Fox, neither herself nor the Lampreys had been real persons"; and she comes further to accept that they have "completely withdrawn from her," excluding her from "the common front they were to present to the police" (32). Earlier, her mind has "seemed to change gear" and she has "found herself thinking of the Lampreys as strangers," with "no knowledge of their reality:" "I have fitted their words and actions into my own idea of them, but my own idea may be quite wrong" (33). She wonders confusedly about "a complete secret reality," momentarily unnerved by a perception of alienation from those she knows and loves. She becomes aware of how little she knows Lord Charles, suddenly seeing him as "an exceedingly remote individual." She realizes that she has "not the smallest inkling of what sort of thoughts went on in his mind"; and she remarks in him "a glint of something" other than his normal "placidity" and "detachment": "a kind of sharpness, so foreign to her idea" of him that she doubts its truth (34). Alleyn's perception of a certain "stylized" qualilty about his courtesy supports the idea that Lord Charles is not exclusively the amiable figure epitomized by "his eyeglass, his smile and his vagueness." Certainly, his brother's murder jolts him from his habitual stance and he speaks "with sudden violence" to his elder children, as if "looking at...and listening to" them "for the first time" (35).

Much of the action is seen in explicit theatrical terms and quickens into "drama" of one kind or another with the arrival of the Wutherwoods. As a comic curtain-raiser, Lord Charles's maternal aunt, the Lady Katherine Lobe, calls unexpectedly. A game old party, who works for charity despite her own relative poverty, she, too, inhabits an odd world of her own. Dame Ngaio presents her playfully, cooking up a minor mystery from her disappearance and contriving for her a conversation at cross purposes with Alleyn; but since she offers so patently the gentlest of comic relief, we never begin to suspect her seriously.

The performance proper begins with the "polite drawing-room comedy" of the opening skirmishes between the Lampreys and the Wutherwoods, complete with "eccentric dowager" in the person of Lady Katherine. Roberta observes that everyone has "begun to pitch their voices like actors and actresses and to use gestures that were a little larger than life" (36). The scene appears to be "building towards some neat and effective climax," with Frid "presenting herself as a lovely and attentive niece" and Henry and the twins listening "enraptured" to Lady Wutherwood. With the crucial interview between Lord Charles and his brother, a "more robust type of drama" is launched, rising to the moment when both men "in unison began to speak and in a moment to shout" (37). Michael reduces the tension by mistiming his entrance as gift-bearer and Lord Wutherwood makes a stormy exit, slamming the door.

Lady Wutherwood is also seen in strong theatrical terms. If Lady Katherine is the benevolent dowager, she is the baleful, sinister one, even more deeply detached from reality. Though once, in Lady Charles's vivid phrase, she had looked "rather spectacular," like "a Gibson Girl who didn't wash very often," she now resesmbles "a white toad," with a sallow, sagging face and "abnormally sunken eyes" with "pin-point pupils" (38). She looks to Lady Katherine like "a lost soul" and seems to Alleyn "a particularly odd-looking woman" creating a sense that "the case had darkened" (39). Her return to the drawing-room strikes "terror to Roberta's heart," her entrance suggestive of "the best traditions of Victorian melodrama." She appears "to have no bones," looking "for all the world as though she dangled by the neck like some ill-managed puppet" (39). With Alleyn her face becomes "a mask of an unlovely Comedy," her laughter "like the cackle of one of the witches in a traditional rendering of *Macbeth*" (41). When she lays a finger across her lips, he is again reminded of *Macbeth* and a further snatch from the opening scene runs through his mind.

Lady Wutherwood is associated with all the macabre elements in the novel, even the murder of her husband, the horror of which she announces and intensifies by her terrible screams. An obsession with witchcraft so dominates her thoughts that she lacks any accessible human personality. She is remote and eerie, "sly," "sidelong," "horridly knowing," seemingly "inconsequent" but, in fact, remarkably consistent, with, like the Lampreys, her own "mad logic." She has two significant themes, one direct, one more elusive, insisting on her right to take possession of her husband's body and conveying a curious sense of having anticipated his death and even of knowing who has killed him. Alleyn penetrates part of her mystery but takes time to assemble the whole picture, so that he is absent from the powerful climactic scene in which Lady Wutherwood moves well beyond melodrama into the horrors of Grand Guignol.

Besides serving as the central issue of the detective element in the novel, Lord Wutherwood's death also contributes obliquely to the theme of unstable personality, since it alters the identity of most of the characters. His brother assumes his title and Lady Charles that of his wife, who, in turn, becomes the dowager. Henry appears dismissive of his new name, describing it as "rather flatulent"; and Michael is horrified by his, regarding "Lord Michael" as "a damn' sight worse" than his existing nickname, "Potty." The tangles of nomenclature in the peerage almost trip Alleyn himself and he is confronted by "the embarrassment of twin titles" (42). Fox, protesting that "The whole thing's lousy with lords and ladies," instructs P. C. Martin to "Stick to Lord Charles" in referring to the father of the Lampreys (43). The servants trip and correct themselves and Martin refers to Henry as "Lord Henry," which is wrong, since he is Lord Rune. When Alleyn sends P. C. Gibson with messages for

Lady Charles and Lady Katherine, he insists he be careful not to call them "Lady Lamprey and Lady Lobe" in error. Even Roberta's aunt enters this particular minefield, by way of a letter reproduced early in the narrative. Her concern lest she may have addressed Lady Charles incorrectly is a comic foreshadowing of the theme of uncertain identity so prevalent later.

All formal detective novels, of course, enshrine the principle of dissimulation and performance: it is the *sine qua non*. The convention demands that someone should kill and yet contrive to show no sign of having done so. *Death of a Peer* is unusual in that Lord Wutherwood's murderer does manifest signs of unease after the event, but, for all that, the novel is formal detective fiction in the classic mold, with no unsettling concern for psychological truth beyond what the form demands. Dame Ngaio meets some of the criteria of the "fair play" detective novel, indicating the central discrepancy on which the murder turns both when it occurs and when it is formally reported, and even drawing attention to it a third time. She is less concerned to place the motive for the murder and reserves a crucial component until late in the narrative.

The circumstances of the murder limit the investigation to a closed circle: of the Lampreys, Lady Wutherwood, Lady Katherine and the Wutherwood servants, the lady's maid Tinkerton, and the chauffeur, Giggle. Alleyn does not waste time trying to prove that Lady Katherine or either of the children murdered Lord Wutherwood, but the rest are naturally regarded as suspects, particularly Stephen and Lady Wutherwood, who accompanied the victim on his descent in the lift. The Lampreys have the obvious motive, but Lady Wutherwood's instability and the lies told by Tinkerton suggest other possibilities. Giggle and Tinkerton appear to be eliminated: she by her left-handedness, he by having disappeared downstairs before the murder. Lord Wutherwood was about to change his will, and Lord Charles has been heard to threaten "to get rid of" him. Alleyn encounters a constable whose naive discussion of *Macbeth* puts "a number of ideas" in his head. In the closing stages, a false killer is insistently incriminated, both by the appearance of what develops and by the cunning deployment of a pronoun. The penultimate chapter includes a second murder and two key revelations, the latter at the end, in the time-honored position.

The action meets admirably the demands of the committed reader of detective fiction, whose primary desire is for intelligent entertainment, with clever contrivance and, at the end, what Margery Allingham called the Element of Satisfaction. Dame Ngaio is accused from time to time of resorting to monotonous formula by relying too obviously on a series of police interviews in the furtherance of her narrative; but the charge is ill sustained by reference to *Death of a Peer*, despite its sequence of eleven such exchanges. Because she proceeds so resourcefully, with such a variety of diversionary tactics, the pattern is never allowed to become obtrusive: it supports the fabric and propels the action, but does so discreetly, without annoying the reader.

Each formal encounter between Alleyn and a witness has its rewards, whether he is coaxing Michael, skirmishing with Lady Charles or being "remarkably crisp" with Tinkerton. He fields whatever is thrown at him: the calculation of Lady Charles, the vagaries of Lady Katherine, the perverse pact beween the twins, the lies of Roberta and Tinkerton. Twice he runs up against something more spectacular in the way of unnerving behavior: when Nanny drives Michael into "a Lamprey rage of some violence" and when Lady Wutherwood starts keening "in the indecent crescendo of hysteria" (44). The entire sequence is richly diverting, each stage both

memorable in itself and yet "a lozenge in the pattern."
" In her early days with the Crime Club, a puff for
Overture to Death described Ngaio Marsh as "a detective
novelist of the first rank," commending her "intelligence and
style," her "fine sense of character and drama" and her "ability
to devise really ingenious plots." *Death of a Peer* continues
to demonstrate all aspects of this claim.

ENDNOTES

1. Ngaio Marsh, *Death of a Peer* (London: Collins, 1941;
   New York: Berkley Publishing Group, 1994), 67. All
   citations refer the the latter edtion. Single words and
   short phrases are not cited.
2. Marsh, 207.
3. Marsh, 10.
4. Marsh, 24
5. Marsh, 35.
6. Marsh, 64.
7. Marsh, 38.
8. Marsh, 60.
9. Marsh, 153-54.
10. Marsh, 37.
11. Marsh, 197.
12. Marsh, 36.
13. Marsh, 138, 221.
14. Marsh, 158.
15. Marsh, 159.
16. Marsh, 111.
17. Marsh, 88.
18. Marsh, 87.

19. Marsh, 209, 294.
20. Marsh, 124.
21. Marsh, 203.
22. Marsh, 100, 216, 217.
23. Marsh, 303.
24. Marsh, 79.
25. Marsh, 219.
26. Marsh, 41.
27. Marsh, 20.
28. Marsh, 103, 204.
29. Marsh, 62.
30. Marsh, 190.
31. Marsh, 186.
32. Marsh, 143-44.
33. Marsh, 101.
34. Marsh, 39.
35. Marsh, 103.
36. Marsh, 52.
37. Marsh, 64.
38. Marsh, 185, 48.
39. Marsh, 161.
40. Marsh, 152.
41. Marsh, 163.
42. Marsh, 108.
43. Marsh, 160.
44. Marsh, 135, 165.

Judgment and Justice in Ngaio Marsh's
Death and the Dancing Footman

by Susan Oleksiw

Detective fiction is the civilized exploration of the most uncivilized act, murder; to this Ngaio Marsh adds social and political criticism, sparked by historical crises that echo our own times. *Death and the Dancing Footman* (1940) is about illusion and deception, of self and others, on many levels--personal, national, international--of the need to create false identities in order to conceal if not erase the true ones given by fate, about the thin membrane that separates each of us from our more primitive selves, and the consequences of the failure to recognize our true natures and rise above our limitations by allegiance to a higher standard in personal integrity.

In the best tradition of the cozy mystery, the novel opens on a Thursday afternoon early in 1940, as Jonathan Royal, local squire, sits in his library anticipating his house party and advising his butler, Caper, to strive for "a feeling of festivity...of positive luxury" (1) while outside the wind grows stronger, the weather colder, and the forces of war more ominous. The first lines signal the contrasts that will be explored throughout the story: the cold outside masked by a false warmth inside.

Chubby and proud of his reputation as a good host, Jonathan
wears thick glasses as he reads the replies to his invitations
(2). In an effort to entertain himself and create a real-life
drama that his friend, Aubrey Mandrake, can shape into a
play, Royal has drawn up his guest list according to an unusual
criterion: each guest has an antipathy to at least one other
guest, thus ensuring that the weekend will have the necessary
sparkle and liveliness (3). Royal first claims he is "an elderly
fogey plagued with the desire to create," then asserts a lofty
desire to aid his friends in facing their secret fears,
subsequently admits his motive is boredom, and later still
confesses to an urge to practice a little psychology (4).
Whatever reason he uses to justify his behavior, he is
admittedly "plotting" and "up to [his] ears in conspiracy" (5),
with no second thoughts about the consequences of his
behavior. Just as his surname tells us his place in the great
social scheme, so his physical description confirms his obvious
character flaw: a moral blindness that will alter the life of
every guest.

Like irresponsible people in power anywhere, Royal
justifies his behavior to himself as well as to others, but as an
English squire he falls back on quintessential English props.
When Aubrey Mandrake, the dramatist guest and ostensible
beneficiary of the anticipated drama, is uncomfortable about
the prospects of the party, Royal reminds him that he has
always been a good host (6). Indeed, Royal's devotion to the
standard of etiquette becomes a recurring theme as crises
deepen and tolerance wanes. At no point, however, does
Royal understand the role of host as anything more than a
duty to provide the best in the way of food and shelter.
Complementing Royal's view of the role of host is his position
as justice of the peace. Although he announces superciliously
to Alleyn that he is a J. P. (7), Royal's behavior during the

twenty-four hours before the murder and the hours after it before Alleyn's arrival is hardly an example of judicial impartiality; he acts more like a prosecuting counsel.

Jonathan Royal's failures are complemented by those of the Compline family. Named after the last of the seven canonical hours, a warning that the family line is coming to its end, the Complines have been neighbors of the Royals for many generations, an old Dorset family whose connection with Jonathan does not for a moment prompt him to reconsider his plans for them (8). Sandra Compline, matron, would be a tragic figure if she weren't thoroughly twisted in her feelings for her two sons. Called by Royal the grande dame of the group, Sandra Compline is a widow whose beauty was destroyed twenty years ago by botched cosmetic surgery undertaken in an effort to hold her philandering husband's attention (9). The cruelly comic look left by the surgery (10) expresses her twisted feelings for her sons, as though fate had shaped her face into a rueful judgment of her life, a drawn-down sad look for William and an exaggerated, loving smile for Nicholas.

Her two sons have equally opposite relations with her: William, the elder, adores her but is ignored; Nicholas, a ladies' man, takes his mother's devotion for granted (11). The brothers have little tolerance for each other. The twisted love within the family defines the relations of its members with outsiders. Chloris Wynne, originally William's girlfriend, is stolen by Nicholas, then breaks off with him over his love affair with another woman, becomes engaged to William , and breaks off with him after he goads Nicholas to take a dip in the pool despite the cold (12).

The remaining member of the old society is Lady Hersey Amblington, a childless widow and a woman without obvious physical flaw by which to measure her character. It is tempting to see in her name an allusion to "herse," meaning one who comes from a railed place, for Lady Hersey's life is certainly circumscribed after her husband's death. She admits to professional jealousy of Madame Lisse, her rival in the beauty business, but refuses to dye her gray hair (13), a sign of her personal honesty, and has no interest in any secrets Jonathan might have uncovered about any of the other guests (14). She is the only member of the old social system who has adapted to modern life, becoming a beauty specialist only after her husband died and left her almost penniless (15). Her willingness to accept changed circumstances puts her at odds with both Jonathan and Sandra. In the end she is disloyal to her class by choosing to judge Dr. Hart on the basis of her own observations rather than the prejudices of her friends.

These three family lines represent the old County society, the social class that governed England and, by extension, the British Empire. Whatever they may have achieved in better days, they have worn themselves out. Jonathan is without an heir, his hopes of continuing the line finally dying when William Compline, unable to develop any affection for Jonathan's niece, broke his engagement with her; William ends his account of this pathetic little tale to Mandrake by reporting that she "went rather queer in the head" (16). By the end of the novel, the Compline line will also come to an end, for William will be dead at his brother's hand and Nicholas will surely be hanged. Lady Hersey, childless and long aware of her cousin Jonathan's "passion for intrigue" and "unholy curiosity" (17), will survive only by abandoning the prejudices of her class, no matter how much compassion she might feel for Jonathan at the end.

Choosing to associate with this class but not of it are two characters. Crippled since birth with a deformed foot that even now causes him acute embarrassment (18), Aubrey

Mandrake is a dramatist who has adopted as his professional pseudonym two names that do not bode well for his future, that in fact suggest no future at all by their suffocating definitions. The name Aubrey, rooted in the Middle English words for "elf" and "power," warns us that he has chosen a childlike, elfish pose, which is reinforced by his arrival in an open car with his hair gratifyingly arranged into "elf-locks," saving him the trouble of doing "the tossing himself" (19). His surname, Mandrake, is a plant known since antiquity for its medicinal properties and its shape as a crooked man, but as Donne once pointed out, the plant is sterile.

The false name is a sign of Mandrake's need to cover his true self, which shames him. The dramatist is crippled by his real name and the humble birth it represents. Born Stanley Footling and raised in his mother's boardinghouse in Dulwich (20), Mandrake cannot accept his identity or reconcile it with his success as a dramatist. Marsh playfully tells us this by the kinds of plays Mandrake composes--plays "of the passion of a pattern-cutter for a headless bust, of a saxophonist who could not perform to his full ability unless his instrument was decked out in tarleton frills, of a lavatory attendant who became a gentleman of the bedchamber," "twelve aspects of one character, all speaking together," and "an experiment in two-dimensional formulism" (21). Mandrake, the surrealist, expresses in his work the disunity, alienation, and disorientation he feels in his life.

Miss Chloris Wynne, "the ingenue" as Royal calls her, arrives engaged to William, and departs in love with Mandrake (22). At first cloying but winning in her attachments to the Compline family, Wynne is without obvious defect, but admits to dying her hair platinum blonde for Nicholas; later she stoutly refuses to change it to her darker, natural shade for Mandrake (23). This is a relatively minor flaw but reflects her less-than-honest emotional life with the brothers until the fateful weekend.

The remaining two characters are the sparks that set alight the dross of Nicholas Compline's baser nature, which ultimately destroys him and his family along with Jonathan Royal's illusions about himself. Dr. Francis Hart and Madame Elise Lisse are Europeans displaced in the social upheaval prior to World War II. Madame Lisse, a beauty specialist who has stolen Lady Hersey's best clients, is a woman of stunning beauty (24). That in itself is a warning that she is a woman obsessed with appearances. She wants no one to know that she is married to Dr. Hart for fear of the effect it would have on her business, and will not give Nicholas Compline any hope for the future if it compromises her financial security and freedom from the terrible poverty she has known (25). Madame Lisse's enjoyment in playing off Nicholas Compline and her husband against each other (26) prods Nicholas to use Dr. Hart as the scapegoat when he decides to murder his brother, William, in order to inherit the family estate and thus be able to provide for Elise. Her name, Elise Lisse, with first and last name nearly identical, suggests duplicity, or that she is without a deeper nature, that no mitigating quality underlies her mercenary interests.

Her name suggests something more. Lisse is derived from the Polish for one who is like a fox or lived near the sign of the fox. Certainly, when the seriousness of the situation becomes apparent to Madame Lisse, she becomes sly, choosing to protect herself by seeking the support of her host to protect her good name while she implicates her husband, carrying out an earlier threat to do whatever is necessary to protect herself (27). Even Inspector Alleyn is awed by her beauty and subjected to her flattery (28). He is offered a self-serving tale that vindicates her and implicates her husband

(29), but in the end it does her no good. Alleyn refuses to see her after Nicholas Compline has been identified as the murderer (30), in what we can surmise to be an attempt to gain assurances that her name will not be linked with Compline's in the newspapers, thereby possibly damaging her reputation.

Dr. Francis Hart differs from all these characters in several ways. An Austrian Jew who has become a naturalized Briton but who still prefers to speak German in private (31), Dr. Hart has embraced his new country with a vengeance by anglicizing his name, adopting English tweeds, and praising the legal system (32), but he arrives at the house party supremely jealous of his wife's attentions to Nicholas Compline and warns her against playing him for a fool (33). His obsession with his wife is the weakness he must overcome, and by the time Inspector Alleyn arrives and gathers the houseguests for a reenactment of the crime, the doctor has done so, acknowledging in conversation the blindness of his passion. In doing so, he also acknowledges that beneath the veneer of the Englishman he is an Austrian peasant (34), and he doesn't sound at all ashamed of it.

Royal has organized his weekend to set sparks among the tinder, giving little regard to the consequences. He begins with Mandrake at dinner Friday evening by putting Nicholas Compline up to mentioning the word "footling" (35); the fear that someone has discovered his name throws Mandrake into a tizzy, but also puts him on the road to self-acceptance, which begins with his savage reference to his crippled foot after he is pushed into a freezing pool, proceeds through a spirited and enlightening talk with Chloris, and concludes with his confession of birth and name to her (36). After confronting his deepest flaw, shame for his social inferiority in addition to his snobbery, he is on the path to a blossoming love with Chloris after she unburdens herself of her shame at her own intellectual shallowness and her behavior with the Compline brothers (37). Before the night of the murder is over, they have found themselves and each other (38). No one else fares as well as these two.

When Mandrake is pushed into the pond in the freezing cold (39), Royal takes the first step away from rational responsibility. Throughout the weekend his behavior becomes progressively arbitrary, his duties as host encompassing little more than handing out drinks, offering food, and appealing to the rules of etiquette. As Mandrake is recovering from his dunking in the pool, Royal tries to persuade him it was a "thoughtless piece of foolery" and is obviously uncomfortable when Nicholas Compline accuses Hart and Hart then accuses Compline (40). Royal also tries to deflect Mandrake's anger by offering the mischievous suggestion that someone really meant to push him, the host, into the pool (41). When the brass Buddha falls on Nicholas's arm and he accuses Hart of rigging the booby trap, the explosion of rage against Hart on all sides is more than Jonathan the host can bear; he keeps everyone under control but just barely (42). Now begins the litany of helplessness repeated by Royal, Mandrake, and others until Alleyn's arrival: "...what in heaven's name am I to do?" (43).

Under the stress of exploding animosities, Royal acts more like a prosecutor than a justice of the peace, a qualification he alludes to erratically like a trump card. He accuses Hart of setting the booby-trap with the brass Buddha, questioning him relentlessly, even drawing on rumors of letters written in anger to Compline before the weekend, then presenting Hart with apparent evidence of his guilt in threatening Compline (44). Royal concludes with a warning and a threat to arrest Hart if anything more serious should happen to Compline (45). After William Compline is found dead, Royal leads a charge to Hart's room, armed with automatic pistols, accuses Hart after waking him from a drugged sleep, pours abuse on him, and leaves the doctor locked in the bedroom (46). When Jonathan questions Thomas the footman after William's murder, only to discover that the young man provides an unbreakable alibi for Dr. Hart, the host is beside himself with anger and frustration (47). "'I won't have that,' Jonathan said loudly, 'there's plenty of time. There must be'" (48). Gone is any pretense of fairness; Jonathan the host can only damn the cleverness of Hart the murderer. Royal continues to object when Hersey later suggests that Hart might be innocent (49).

Jonathan Royal is at his worst when he is accusing Hart of murdering Compline, flying into a rage, assuming guilt, and repeating over and over the phrase "in my home" (50), as though the greater offense were the breach of etiquette, not the taking of a life. A man with the social position, power, and wealth that his surname implies, Jonathan Royal feels free to play with his guests' lives, yet falls apart when a genuine crisis arises, unable to rise above petty prejudices and self-interest. He is a king playing with the lives of his courtiers, revealing just how shallow and selfish he really is. He exercises power without responsibility.

It is a favorite device of Marsh to temper the young through a murder and its investigation, and both Mandrake and Wynne reach maturity as they go on to draw their own conclusions about the crimes. Their private shames safely acknowledged after the incident in the pool, Mandrake and Wynne find themselves dissociating their views from their host's and taking on greater responsibility. Mandrake hates Royal's armed interrogation of Hart, the suspected murderer, disagrees with Royal's insistence that Hart must have found a way to carry out the murder despite the footman's evidence, takes on the task of writing a summary of events, and discovers on the drive to collect Inspector Alleyn a new pleasure in the physical challenge of getting the car through snowdrifts and across flooded hollows (51), his crippled foot completely forgotten. His behavior in this scene is a long way from that of his arrival in an open sports car designed to produce an artistic effect. The change in his character is noted by both Agatha Troy and her husband, Alleyn (52).

The shallowness of many of the guests is symbolized by their concern with physical beauty. Madame Lisse is a beauty specialist and enjoys taking Lady Hersey's upper class clients; Sandra Compline ruined her beauty in a desperate attempt to use cosmetic surgery to save her marriage; and Dr. Hart turned from general practice to cosmetic surgery years ago (53). The concern with appearances is introduced by Jonathan Royal, who orders his butler to strive for "a feeling of festivity, of anticipation,...of positive luxury" (54). He orders "large fires in the bedrooms," has the furniture dressed in the slip covers that are "summer-time uniforms," and arranges large bouquets of flowers for each guest (55), all this while a snowstorm builds outside. Though Royal sees the decorated guest rooms and lavish arrangements as backdrops for his guests' encounters with each other (and their secret fears), they are in fact his own beauty makeover. He dresses up Highfold as it might have appeared in its heyday, before World War I, just as Lady Hersey's and Madame Lisse's clients struggle to recapture the beauty of their youth.

The false spring within Highfold contrasts with the weather outside. As the story opens Royal is in his library planning his weekend when Caper, his butler, enters and comments, "It's a dark afternoon" (56). Outside are wind and sleet; by the time Royal has explained all to Mandrake and both men are ready to retire for the night, the weather has worsened to "a deadly cold" (57). Snow falls during the night, and the day dawns dark and cold (58). After William bets that Nicholas won't take a dip in the pool, the snow begins to fall, only a few flakes at first, then in earnest after dinner and during the Charter game in which Nicholas finds a threat and warning allegedly from Dr. Hart (59). The sunshine of the following morning gives way to more snow after Mandrake's fall into the pool; the snow continues to pile up for the rest of the day (60). The comment by one character or another that it's snowing harder than ever (61) punctuates the rising animosity among the guests until after the murder and after Thomas the footman gives his evidence, effectively providing Dr. Hart with an alibi (62). Only then does it begin to rain (63), foreshadowing the end of false accusation and deceit. In the following scene, the characters decide to try to reach Inspector Alleyn, who is staying nearby (64). After this decision, the rain cleanses Cloudyfold and the Highfold estate.

Marsh's characterization of the British ruling classes might be taken as no more than the skeptical views of a former colonial. As a New Zealander, she might understandably withhold approval of the ruling classes of Great Britain, but she provides a broader context for her views on the behavior of Jonathan Royal and the Compline brothers. Royal might be living in a grand country house recalling the heyday of the British Empire, but such a lifestyle suggesting superiority is an illusion, just as Royal's role as host is an illusion and a veil for a meddling, cruel character.

The falseness of Royal's personal superiority is highlighted by the smoking room, the scene of the murder; the room has "remained unaltered since [Jonathan's] father died" (65), with the exception of the addition of a telephone and radio. A "collection of sporting prints [is] flanked by a

collection of weapons and by fading groups of Jonathan and
his Cambridge friends in the curious photographic postures
of the nineties." A complete trout rod and reel hang above
the fireplace (66). Inspector Alleyn gives us a more
comprehensive view, carefully noting the collection of
weapons hanging above the desk: "a Malay kriss, a
boomerang, a Chinese dagger, and a Javanese knife; the fruits,
thought Alleyn, of some Royal tour through the East to
Oceania" (67). The Maori mere, the murder weapon, lies on
the floor. Above the mantelpiece are a rod and reel and
nearby a photograph recording the "hunting" weapon's great
achievement: a four-and-a-half pounder caught from Pen-
Felton Reach in 1900 (68). The mighty empire that stretched
around the world, in which divergent tribes and nations were
linked together under one governing power, is reduced to a
selection of weapons, with the British represented by a fishing
rod. No single weapon is greater than any other.

   The weapons do not seem out of place in the English
manor house, for despite the veneer of civilization, the squire
and his guests are barely a crisis away from their primitive
ancestors. Mandrake senses this on Friday evening, after
Nicholas has been injured by the falling Buddha. Everyone is
now alarmed and most of the guests have withdrawn into
separate groups convinced of Dr. Hart's malicious intent. As
the tension mounts before Mandrake and Jonathan confront
Dr. Hart, Mandrake has a passing vision: "When he saw Dr.
Hart the fancy crossed Mandrake's mind that Highfold was full
of solitary figures crouched over fires" (69). The passing
thought is a startling one, for it conjures up images of
tribesmen squatting around evening campfires and soldiers
kneeling around theirs, each one waiting through the night,
before the next day of hunting or battle. Under the threat of
danger, primitive urges return, and the thin layer of

civilization, the topsoil of culture and etiquette, is blown away by inchoate fears and hatreds. Royal and his friends do not represent a superior culture but rather one tribe among many, and this equality is symbolized by the inclusion of the rod and reel among the array of hunting tools hanging on the walls. If this were Marsh's only point, it would be sobering enough, and understandable for the year in which the novel was written, before the extended war in Europe exploded. But Marsh does not choose to stop here. Through one character in particular, she indicates the only way to transcend our smallness as human beings. Marsh shrewdly relies on the prejudices of her time to create in Dr. Hart an "almost arrogantly foreign figure" (70) who serves as a litmus test for open-mindedness and tolerance. As the danger increases, men and women are forced back into themselves and reveal their true characters: some sink deep into their tribal natures, and to them Dr. Hart seems more and more sinister; others grapple with the challenge of a murderer among them and throw off preconceived views, struggling to understand accurately circumstances and their fellow guests.

In his early remarks to Mandrake, Royal introduces Hart as "the heavy," a naturalized Briton who was originally Viennese and a plastic surgeon (71). When the host goes on to describe the rumors of his association with Madame Lisse, prejudice against Dr. Hart deepens. Madame Lisse refers her clients to him for surgery, and Royal reports that the doctor has been seen

> leaving Madame Lisse's flat at a most compro-
> mising hour; that he presented to an exciting
> degree the mien of a clandestine lover, his hat
> drawn over his brows, his cloak (he wears a
> cloak) pulled about his face. They say that he

has been observed to scowl most formidably
at the mention of Nicholas Compline (72).

We are given the picture of a furtive, threatening figure whose foreignness is underscored by pointed reference to the cloak. The picture borders on the ludicrous. Royal's reference to a Tyrolese cloak with a hood that Hart gave him does not ameliorate our reactions: "He has presented me with one. I wear it frequently" (73). We must now regard Hart as menacing or comical.

Our first view of Dr. Hart is not designed to liberate the reader from Royal's introduction but rather to complicate it. While driving towards Cloudyfold with Madame Lisse, Hart insists he be allowed to speak German despite the current antipathy for the language, since he is a "naturalized Austrian" and everyone knows he despises the Nazis (74). He acquiesces to Lisse's request, nevertheless, and in English continues his argument about Compline (75). His jealousy is obvious (76), reinforcing the image of the possessive, secret lover. During the coming weekend, Hart looks more and more like an angry, foreign bully while Nicholas emerges as the slightly immature but nonetheless attractive young soldier, continuing the play on cultural sympathies. During the first evening at cocktails, for example, Hart is formal and polite to Nicholas (77), behavior that is understood to be admirable indeed when we learn later that Madame Lisse is Hart's wife, but perception of his perfectly correct behavior on that first evening is undermined by Mandrake's observation that the man has eyelids that resemble "those of a lizard" (78).

The biased presentation of Dr. Hart prevents us from appreciating the depth of his character in comparison to that of his fellow guests when he is the first to make a confession of a past failing, one that is far more serious than the personal hurdles the other characters face. Immediately after the cocktail party, Dr. Hart confesses to Madame Lisse that he is responsible for Mrs. Compline's grotesque appearance (79). He admits to a lifelong regret for what he has done, and no amount of coaxing by Madame Lisse will persuade him to deny his culpability (80). It is here that we first understand the significance of his name--he alone has the heart to sympathize with another and to remain honest. And yet, the gossip offered by Jonathan and the observations by Mandrake tempt the reader to condemn Hart for what he did twenty years ago, a reaction that would not have occurred for any other character--for example, Lady Hersey making the same admission.

Marsh carefully lays out the evidence of Hart's character, often in contrast to Nicholas's, and yet in the coming hours the other guests are willingly misled by their own prejudices. Rather than consider the reasonable explanations offered by Dr. Hart, Royal and the others at the manor stubbornly insist that Hart is the culprit. The servants Caper and Mrs. Pouting, the former ironically and the latter aptly named, are the most obvious (81), but Alleyn observes early in the investigation that the same convention of blaming the foreigner has made its way into Mandrake's notes (82).

Initially, there is no doubt in Royal's and the other guests' minds that Dr. Hart is guilty of the two assaults--the first against Mandrake and the second against Nicholas Compline--the threat against Nicholas in the Charter game, and the murder of William (83), despite Hart's countervailing conduct in his offer to attend to Mandrake and Compline, and his attempt to save Sandra Compline when she is found comatose from a drug overdose (84). The doctor is meticulously correct in his advice on protecting the murder scene and finding someone to observe the victim and forthright about his limitations as a doctor when he offers to help Mrs. Compline (85), but indefatigable in his efforts to save her. His devotion to his patient finally convinces Lady Hersey of his innocence (86).

The climax is threaded with irony. Dr. Hart, a refugee from the poison of Naziism spreading across Europe, has taken refuge in a land whose people profess a different philosophy, only to find himself the object of baseless accusations of assault and murder after a campaign of smirking innuendo. Yet he works tirelessly to save the life of a woman who would sacrifice her life to protect her son from a charge of murder, or willingly implicate an innocent man.

At no point does Dr. Hart shirk from the truth of his responsibility for Mrs. Compline's disfigurement, or from what he feels obligated to do as a doctor. His sureness contrasts with the uncertainty and confusion of everyone else. As soon as it is evident that circumstances are escalating beyond anyone's control, Jonathan offers a lament that becomes a litany: "...what in heaven's name am I to do?" (87). Though a J. P., Jonathan understands only the mechanical aspects of the position; he protects Sandra Compline's suicide note for the police (88), but accepts unquestioningly Nicholas's accusations of Dr. Hart for threatening him in the Charter game, attempting to shove him in the pool, and booby-trapping his door (89). When Thomas the footman provides an unbreakable alibi for Dr. Hart, the host becomes enraged (90). He continues to object when Hersey suggests that Dr. Hart might be innocent (91); Jonathan's is a blindness of terrible consequences.

The lord of the manor, justice of the peace, mastermind behind the show is completely unable to figure out a solution to extricate himself and his guests from a nightmare of his own devising. Like the photographs of him and his

Cambridge friends hanging in the smoking room (92), the wisdom of his class has long since faded. The old society that once ruled the world (or at least thought it did) is reduced to a middle-aged man playing parlor games with his friends' lives; the bearer of a tradition that once claimed to offer fair treatment to all under its sway is incapable of rational judgment or even of withholding judgment until the proper authorities arrive. When Jonathan's house party gets out of hand, all he can do is fret about what he should do and fall back on the hollow appeal to etiquette, a standard he has breached since the creation of the guest list. The signal concern of the lord of the manor has shrunk from justice to party manners.

When the bearers of English tradition fail in the crisis, it is left to Dr. Hart--the foreigner in speech, heritage, and religion--to recover what distinguishes and redeems them. Lady Hersey comments on Dr. Hart's presence of mind as they work to save Sandra.

> "You mean that I am not afraid," said Dr. Hart,
> who was again stooping over his patient. "You
> are right. Lady Hersey, I am an Austrian refugee
> and a Jew who has become a naturalized Briton.
> I have developed what I believe you would call
> a good nose for justice. Austrian justice, Nazi
> justice and English justice. I have learned when
> to be terrified and when not to be terrified. I am
> a kind of thermometer for terror. At this moment
> I am quite normal. I do not believe I shall be
> found guilty of a murder I did not commit" (93).

This is our first insight into Dr. Hart's thinking; at every earlier moment we have seen his passionate, angry reactions to accusations, his obsession with his wife, but never his inner logic. In a single quiet moment, he links one domestic murder to the wholesale slaughter of the embattled plains of war stretching around the world, putting into perspective not only small and grand behavior but also real and imaginary recourse from danger. Jonathan may be the squire who has become a fool squandering his heritage and betraying his principles, but justice is not dependent on him or on any other single person. Justice in a nation of equitable laws is not arbitrary, and so Dr. Hart bides his time.

Dr. Hart is not an entirely admirable character, however. Marsh has given him unattractive traits: his anger and jealousy, his slightly pompous air and impeccable courtesy that make him seem rigid, his apparent desire to ingratiate himself with his new countrymen expressed in his gift of a cloak to Royal, and his arrogant bearing. All these qualities of personality complicate his deeper character of wisdom, honesty, and generosity born partly of experience.

Dr. Hart is not a naive optimist either. Whereas Jonathan confuses his personal interests with his professional position, Hart recognizes the possibly conflicting but overriding requirements of officialdom and the responsibilities of the ordinary citizen to comply with them. When Alleyn arrives, the doctor asks him to make a record of his treatment, for he readily acknowledges he is in a precarious position (94), but this formality conceals the one act of charitable feeling among all of the guests, his willingness to risk his own reputation to save Sandra (95). Moreover, unlike the others, Dr. Hart seeks to atone for his conduct (96), a striking contrast to Jonathan Royal, who is still vituperating about the doctor's "effrontery" in violating his hospitality by committing murder in his home (97).

As harsh as Marsh's judgment is, she does not condemn all members of British society. Lady Hersey, though she has been appalled by her cousin's behavior, manages compassion for both her cousin and herself (98), and we think Royal might actually have learned his lesson. More importantly, after the arrest of Nicholas Compline, Hart makes a speech offstage to Alleyn, "causing him acute embarrassment by many references to the courtesy and integrity of the British police" (99), reminding us once again that men and women loyal to a principle embodied in law raise the level of everyone in society.

This passage suggests that Marsh felt very strongly about a law free of the bias of its upholders. Even after several readings, the passage seems too obvious after the graceful speech of Dr. Hart to Lady Hersey when they are working on Sandra Compline (100). There, the comment on the integrity of British justice is an honest sentiment, its expression simple, natural, unforced, the logical cresting of the waves of emotions that have been building all weekend. At the end, the comment seems awkward and forced, an expression of principle that Marsh seemed determined to make, perhaps driven by the horrors building on the Continent. However its expression is viewed, the principle is an important one for Marsh.

The war is a minor theme throughout the novel, a background noise that cannot be forgotten. Jonathan ignores it except for drawing his blackout screens; William Compline accepts it as one more duty he automatically fulfills whether he enjoys it or not, its danger taken for granted; Nicholas finds it a threat until he is sure he will avoid combat, and the war thereafter becomes a talking point, an opportunity to swagger, or a convenient excuse when he needs one (101). Madame Lisse considers it a reminder of the harsh life she has escaped

(102). Only Dr. Hart sees it as an opportunity to serve those who truly need the care of a surgeon, not vain women growing old (103).

The introduction of the war into an admittedly "cosy little murder," in Alleyn's words, allows Marsh to repeat her views on individual justice and responsibility. In lines reminiscent of the close of *Love's Labors Lost*, Alleyn says:

> "I believe that in a year's time we shall look
> back on these frozen weeks as on a strangely
> unreal period. Does it seem odd to you, Fox,
> that we should be here so solemnly tracking
> down one squalid little murderer, so laboriously
> using our methods to peer into two deaths,
> while over our heads are stretched the legions
> of guns? It's as if we stood on the edge of a
> cracking landslide, swatting flies."
>
> The stolid Fox replies simply, "It's our job."
> (104)

And in this response are the two spheres of death linked. The investigation of a murder in a country house is as important for the maintenance of justice as the defense of a nation in a world at war. The same principle of pursuing justice above all other considerations, setting aside personal interests, informs both activities. Just as the torch lighting the path of social responsibility passes from Jonathan's generation to Mandrake's, so the sphere of that responsibility spreads from the small world of the individual, be it town or manor house, to a larger sphere of the nation and the world. The petty desires of individuals erupt into the same passions that lead nations into war, and both call forth the same meticulous justice.

In the conduct of Dr. Hart and the transformation of Lady Hersey, Aubrey Mandrake, and Chloris Wynne, we have what John Gardner calls moral fiction. Though he did not consider the average detective novel capable of rising to the standards he sets for literature, *Death and the Dancing Footman* nevertheless offers what Gardner considers the mark of aesthetic integrity: her novel depicts "responsible humanness" (105), and offers an affirmation of life and an exploration of responsible behavior in difficult times.

ENDNOTES

1. Ngaio Marsh, *Death and the Dancing Footman* (Harmondsworth: Penguin Books), 1949, 11. All references are to this edition.
2. Marsh, 9, 23, 10-11.
3. Marsh, 16-17.
4. Marsh, 15, 59, 60, 118.
5. Marsh, 14.
6. Marsh, 23.
7. Marsh, 242.
8. Marsh, 17.
9. Marsh, 17-18.
10. Marsh, 30.
11. Marsh, 20.
12. Marsh, 91.
13. Marsh, 41-42.
14. Marsh, 60.
15. Marsh, 22.

16. Marsh, 53-54.
17. Marsh, 59.
18. Marsh, 13.
19. Marsh, 13.
20. Marsh, 76.
21. Marsh, 12, 26, 31.
22. Marsh, 23, 20, 316.
23. Marsh, 21, 204.
24. Marsh, 41, 46.
25. Marsh, 39, 119.
26. Marsh, 39.
27. Marsh, 234-35, 263.
28. Marsh, 265, 267.
29. Marsh, 268.
30. Marsh, 307.
31. Marsh, 232, 38.
32. Marsh, 53, 46, 232.
33. Marsh, 39, 41.
34. Marsh, 299.
35. Marsh, 60, 62-63.
36. Marsh, 81, 85, 94, 111.
37. Marsh, 111-13.
38. Marsh, 157.
39. Marsh, 81.
40. Marsh, 85, 87, 88-89.
41. Marsh, 90.
42. Marsh, 125.
43. Marsh, 126.
44. Marsh, 140-43.
45. Marsh, 144.
46. Marsh, 158, 161, 165.
47. Marsh, 173-74.
48. Marsh, 178.

49. Marsh, 200.
50. Marsh, 165.
51. Marsh, 159, 168-69, 180-81, 193.
52. Marsh, 213.
53. Marsh, 39, 18, 198.
54. Marsh, 11.
55. Marsh, 11, 26-27.
56. Marsh, 9.
57. Marsh, 11, 25.
58. Marsh, 26.
59. Marsh, 44, 70, 72.
60. Marsh, 77, 91, 96.
61. Marsh, 99, 109, 126, 138, 139, 164.
62. Marsh, 173-74.
63. Marsh, 175.
64. Marsh, 177.
65. Marsh, 28.
66. Marsh, 28.
67. Marsh, 236-37.
68. Marsh, 238.
69. Marsh, 139.
70. Marsh, 306.
71. Marsh, 23.
72. Marsh, 24.
73. Marsh, 24.
74. Marsh, 38.
75. Marsh, 38-39.
76. Marsh, 40.
77. Marsh, 46.
78. Marsh, 49.
79. Marsh, 55.
80. Marsh, 55-56.
81. Marsh, 259, 261-62.

82. Marsh, 213.
83. Marsh, 88, 123, 75, 156.
84. Marsh, 87-88, 122, 191.
85. Marsh, 164, 198.
86. Marsh, 200.
87. Marsh, 126, 137-38, 155, 165.
88. Marsh, 191, 241.
89. Marsh, 128.
90. Marsh, 173-74, 178.
91. Marsh, 200-01.
92. Marsh, 28.
93. Marsh, 232.
94. Marsh, 244.
95. Marsh, 245.
96. Marsh, 246.
97. Marsh, 241.
98. Marsh, 177, 316.
99. Marsh, 305.
100. Marsh, 242.
101. Marsh, 9-10, 33, 19-20, 100-02.
102. Marsh, 119.
103. Marsh, 306.
104. Marsh, 297. I am indebted to my friend, Dr. Sara
     Leigh Carney-Hawkins for the allusion to
     Shakespeare's play.
105. John Gardner, *On Becoming a Novelist* (n.p.:
     Perennial, 1985), 50.

Short Fiction

Marsh's Miniatures: An Examination
of Ngaio Marsh's Short Mystery Stories

by Douglas G. Greene

Ngaio Marsh said that she was "no dab at the short story" (1), and most critics seem to agree with her. Marsh has been fortunate to have become the subject of two excellent books, a biography by Margaret Lewis and a critical study by Kathryne Slate McDorman, but neither pays much attention to her short stories. McDorman's analysis of Marsh's works does not mention the short stories at all (2), and Margaret Lewis is not enthusiastic about most of them:

> Ngaio never found the short story form to be
> congenial, probably because her favored method
> of starting a story meant beginning with a group
> of characters, and exploring how they interact.
> Such a technique requires time, and the short
> story needs a more direct approach (3).

The two magisterial critics, Jacques Barzun and Wendell Hertig Taylor, examine only one of Marsh's short stories, "Death on the Air," and they are not pleased: "It all goes to show that one talent does not imply another" (4).

On the other hand, Frederic Dannay called her second short story, "I Can Find My Way Out, " "suave, intelligent, and amusing" (5), and when her short stories were finally gathered together in 1989 in *The Collected Short Fiction of Ngaio Marsh*, the book was a popular success. The first edition was quickly followed by a book-club version (which the Mystery Guild used as a premium to attract new memberships), then by a trade paperback which included a story discovered after the publication of the first edition, and then by an edition specially produced for the bargain-book counters. Total sales of all four printings approached 28,000 copies, and by the time this essay is published, yet another edition will be available, a rack-sized paperback retitled *Alleyn and Others*.

In looking at Ngaio Marsh's short detective and mystery fiction as a whole, I find that her short stories vary greatly in quality, but that she could (and did) write some excellent tales and, in fact, they avoid one of the few problems that appear in many of her longer works. She often began her novels rather as though she were drawing back the curtain on a stage play, with the main characters already posed and ready to play their ordained roles. The problem with this approach is that Marsh sometimes introduced so many characters in that opening scene that the reader, without a program to guide him or her, has to make an effort to sort them all out. (The old Pocket Books editions, with their cast of characters listed at the beginning, are especially useful in reading Marsh's novels.) The shorter form, however, forced Marsh to have a smaller cast of characters who are more sharply, if less subtly, defined than in her novels.

As a young woman during the 1920's, Marsh tried to write an ambitious New Zealand novel, but she completed only two chapters. Her main efforts were focused on what she described as "verses, articles and short stories, some of which found local publication" (6). Probably as a novice writer she chose the short form for a reason given by fellow detective-story author, John Dickson Carr:

> We did not want merely to "write." When a
> person says that, he often means only that he
> wants to dream. No; we were more practical;
> we wanted to write a story. Since it would
> have been too big an undertaking to write a
> long story, we simply had a go at what we
> considered a short story (7).

Many of Marsh's first stories were never published and the manuscripts lost—"and well lost, too," Marsh later recalled. But in her autobiography she gives the plot of one of them, a story she said was inspired by E. M. Forster and possibly by Walter de la Mare. It was a supernatural tale that sounds more effective than Marsh claimed: A traveller enters a mysterious road leading to an enchanted valley and eventually comes upon "a submerged house." Its owner is a woman whom he believes to be injured, since she lies on a couch, her body covered with multi-colored silks. She gives him a room for the night, and that evening he wakes to the sound of wings. Looking out his window, the traveler sees the woman flying away "with great upward sweeps between him and the stars" over the steep sides of the valley. Marsh was later pleased that she had lost the typescript, since she feared "I might find it foolish now and that, I suddenly realize, is a sensation I might not enjoy" (8). Certainly the story seems to have been derivative, but it probably was not foolish.

Marsh's apprentice tales that found publication mostly appeared in a New Zealand newspaper, *The Christchurch Sun*, which sponsored an annual literary competition. The newspaper is not available through American libraries, but Margaret Lewis describes a story called "The Gold Escort," which won a third prize in December 1926. It is a standard supernatural story that, clumsily, ends by denying the supernatural. A miner falls asleep, and a ghostly gang persuades him to enter their coach, which then careens out of control down a mountainside. Just as destruction seems certain, the miner wakes and finds it was all a dream. "Moonshine," reprinted in Warwick Lawrence's anthology *Yours and Mine, Stories by Young New Zealanders* (New Plymouth, New Zealand: Avery, 1936), is a sentimental tale of a child at Christmas. As Margaret Lewis implies, it is more interesting as a biographical piece about Marsh's lifelong love of Christmas than it is as a story (9).

The best of Marsh's early stories is another ghost tale, this one without a rational resolution or, indeed, any resolution at all. "The Figure Quoted" first appeared in *The Christchurch Sun*, Christmas 1927; it became Marsh's first publication in England when it was reprinted in O. N. Gillespie's *New Zealand Short Stories* (London: Dent, 1930); and it was collected in the second edition of *The Collected Short Fiction of Ngaio Marsh* (New York: International Polygonics, 1991). Although it has some problems in tone (Marsh does not make the jocular and the supernatural fit together), it is an impressive performance. An auctioneer named Batey deals in used and, often, useless material, including a marble basin with a platform "where once upon a time a stone nymph must have sat" (10). To his astonishment, two bidders push up the price of the valueless basin: a man who seems quite determined to have the item, and a woman who, for a while, is obscured from Batey's view by sunlight on the top of a flight of stairs. As she "floated, rather then walked" to the bannister, however, Batey suddenly sees that she is wearing nothing at all—and that no one else notices.

The man wins the bidding, and walks toward the naked woman, but she has become a statue. He picks her up and places her on the empty platform of the basin. Marsh gives no explanation how or why Batey thought that she was alive and participating in the bidding for the basin, or why the man wanted the basin and statue so desperately.

Some day a scholar should investigate the influence of the supernatural on Marsh's fiction. Did the moodiness, the feeling of seeing something through a mist, that seems to have been a part of her unpublished de la Mare/Forster story reflect her feeling of being separated from her British homeland because of her Colonial birth? Did reading the lyrical descriptive passages in such writers as de la Mare influence Marsh's own later ability to describe the countryside in such books as *Clutch of Constables*? Kathryne McDorman rightly attributes the vividness of her writing, at least in part, to her painter's eye: "Her training as a painter affected her writing, endowing it with a visual clarity seldom found in detective fiction and nowhere as consistently as in Marsh's novels" (11). I would add that this clarity also has a lyricism that is due as much to de la Mare as to the painter's palette.

When Marsh became a professional writer, however, she left the realm of the ghostly for the rationality of the detective story. Probably shortly after she wrote her first novel, *A Man Lay Dead*, Marsh decided to try her hand at a detective novelette. During the 1930's, several of the major British fiction magazines were still active, including *The Strand* and *The Windsor*, but it is not known whether she submitted anything to these journals. Her story, *Death on the Air*, was published in the December 1934 issue of a downgrade competitor, *The Grand Magazine*, with a co-author, A. Drummond Sharpe (12), who apparently appeared and disappeared solely for the occasion. Nothing seems to have been recorded about him in standard sources, and in all reprints of the story his name has been omitted. "Death on the Air" is a typically artificial closed circle detective story of the period, with almost everyone having a motive and opportunity to kill the thoroughly despicable victim, one Septimus Tonks. Alleyn eventually forces someone whose motive we had not previously suspected into doing the right thing in good 1930's manner by committing suicide. Unfortunately, how Alleyn knew he was guilty is never explained.

As Inspector Alleyn's second published case, "Death on the Air" has some interesting features. Like many of Marsh's novels of the 1930's and the 1940's, the murder method is unusual, though perhaps not so striking as the murderer who slides down the bannister, or who dispatches his victims with guns rigged inside pianos. In the novelette, Tonks is killed when someone replaces the bakelite knobs on his radio with metal ones taken from some convenient curtains rods. Tonks is thereby "galvanized," that is, electrocuted. Alleyn remains the Bright Young Tec of the early novels. In *A Man Lay Dead* he actually says, "You've guessed my boyish secret. I've been given a murder to solve—aren't I a lucky little detective?" In "Death on the Air" he announces, "Fox! A clue. A very palpable clue!" (13). Bailey is properly mystified by what Alleyn immediately understands about the case, and so is Fox (14). And Alleyn's remark, "I have no imagination" (15) may indicate that H. C. Bailey's Reggie Fortune was as much an influence on Alleyn's gestation as was Dorothy L. Sayers's Lord Peter Wimsey. Whatever the case, Marsh's first short detective story gives no impression of Alleyn's character except that, like most fictional detectives of 1930's Britain, he knows more than his colleagues and like Fortune and Wimsey, he occasionally speaks piffle.

Alleyn is much more interesting in Marsh's next short story. Lewis indicates that Marsh wrote several short works during the 1940's, but most of them were not published until many years later (16). The only one to appear during that decade was "I Can Find My Way Out," written for *Ellery Queen's Mystery Magazine*'s first annual short story contest. Published in the August 1946 issue, it won third prize. The story is much more smoothly told and plotted than "Death on the Air," and Alleyn is a believable character, who actually has some evidence for identifying the murderer. The tale is marred only by another outré murder device, this one involving the peculiar habits of British gas heaters of the 1940's. The story is set among a group of actors, and like a play it is structured in several clearly delineated scenes. Roderick and Troy Alleyn's friend Lord Michael Lamprey has agreed, through a strange series of circumstances, to deliver a costume to the theater. When he tries on the false beard, the leading lady faints. Having hurried backstage, Lamprey finds a card with Alleyn's name on it and so, being a playful young chap, identifies himself as Inspector Alleyn. None of this is sorted out before a dissolute actor named Canning Cumberland is asphyxiated in his dressing-room in the middle of the play. Alleyn shows up, rescues the properly chastened young nobleman, and finds out who decided Cumberland's death to have been necessary. In the climactic scene, Alleyn is hit in the face by the murderer. "In a way, sir," says one of the police officers, "it's handy when they have a smack at you. You can pull them in nice and straightforward." "Quite," Alleyn replies nursing his jaw (17). This brief passage indicates how Alleyn had become much more human since the early novels, but the strength of "I Can Find My Way Out" is that in a relatively small number of words, Marsh creates the mood of a theater on opening night: the tensions, the jealousies, the hopes, and the fears.

Marsh waited sixteen years before publishing another short story. "The Cupid Mirror," a short-short which first appeared in an anthology, *The Drugged Cornet* (New York:

Dutton, 1972), is probably one of the stories that Marsh wrote much earlier. The narrator, Lord John Challis, tells of events that occurred in 1907, and the feeling of the tale is Edwardian. A demanding old woman who bullies her niece and accepts the fawning behavior of her mercenary doctor died suddenly at her meal in a restaurant. Was the death accidental, or did the doctor kill her for her money, or the niece to escape from dependence upon her? The answer is that another character committed the murder because he was simply fed up with the old woman. "Exasperation," Lord John explains, "may be the motive of many unsolved crimes" (18). Charmingly amoral, "The Cupid Mirror" benefits from a small cast of characters and a single setting, as well as from the urbane personality of the narrator. "Male snobs," Marsh told an interviewer, "have always fascinated me" (19).

"Chapter and Verse," first published in *Ellery Queen's Mystery Magazine*, March 1973, has been called Marsh's best short story (20), and it is certainly an accomplished affair. The Alleyns are living in the village of Little Copplesford. By this time a Superintendent, Alleyn is in London when Troy meets Mr. Bates, a bookseller from New Zealand, who carries with him a huge Bible with references to a family called the Hadets. The Bible records that the Hadets, several of whom had died in 1779, once lived in Little Copplesford, but, oddly enough, there is no local evidence of their existence. The matter seems amusing until someone pushes the inoffensive Bates from the church tower. It seems inconceivable that murder would be committed to discourage queries about a family dead for two hundred years—and which, in any event, may never have existed at all. Alleyn returns from London in time to identify the cleverly concealed murderer. Marsh once wrote in a letter that "unknotting of clues has never been one of my talents" (21). Whether or not that was the situation with her novels, Marsh does an expert job in "Chapter and Verse" in handling a traditional detective story gambit, the concealed message, which in this tale is not even known to be a message until Alleyn unravels it. As in "The Cupid Mirror," a small cast in a confined place, in this case a village with an assortment of local characters, brings the story to life; and Marsh uses preconceptions about village types as a way of misdirecting the reader.

"A Fool about Money" is an entertaining but inconsequential short-short of around 1000 words. According to Margaret Lewis, Marsh had drafted the story many years earlier and decided to revise it in 1973, when *Esquire* commissioned her and other writers to produce some short stories for one thousand dollars each. After Marsh submitted "A Fool about Money" however, *Esquire* backed out of the deal, cancelled all the stories, and decided not to pay Marsh and the others. This decision brought down the wrath of Marsh's United States agent, Dorothy Olding of Harold Ober Associates, on the heads of *Esquire*'s editors, and Marsh was paid. The story eventually appeared in the December 1974 issue of *Ellery Queen's Mystery Magazine.* Lewis records that Marsh had misgivings about the story (22), and in fact it is little more than an anecdote. "A Fool about Money" concerns an overbearing husband who makes himself the life of every party by endlessly retelling an embarrassing story about his wife Hersey: "Where money is concerned, my poor Hersey—and she won't mind my saying so, will you darling?—is the original dumbbell" (23). He then regales the audience with the story of how he left a fiver for Hersey to take on a train trip, how she became convinced that another woman had stolen it from her, how she managed to retrieve the missing note, and how at the end he had wired her that she had left the fiver at home. It turns out, however, that the husband rather than the wife had made the mistake, and the story ends with Hersey having "the glint of victory in her eyes"

(24). *Esquire*, with its largely male audience, was probably not the market for this story, and it would be interesting to know whether Hersey's husband was created as a contrast to the sensitivity of Roderick Alleyn.

Marsh wrote her final short story, "Morepork," in response to a request from Julian Symons, President of the Detection Club, to contribute a story about a jury to a Detection Club anthology called *Verdict of Thirteen*, published in 1978. The Detection Club had as its members the most important writers of pure detective stories. Marsh had been invited as a guest to at least one meeting in the late 1930's, but because she could not regularly attend its meetings in London, she did not become a member until 1974 (25). By the time that the story was published, Marsh was 83 years old, but it is one of her finest tales. Once again the story emphasizes a small number of people in a single, enclosed setting. An ill-matched group of campers is stranded in a forest on New Zealand's South Island: "Beech bush, emerging from the night, was threaded with mist. The voices of the nearby creek and the more distant Wainui River, in endless colloquy with stones and boulders, filled the intervals between bird song" (26). The party contains a bird lover named Caley Bridgeman, Bridgeman's stepson who hates him, his wife who prefers other men, as well as a taxidermist who twists the necks of birds. When Bridgeman is murdered after setting up a tape recorder to capture the voice of a bird called the Morepork, everyone is suspect. Also stranded is a party of deer hunters, including a barrister and a doctor. Since there are no police to report to, the group decides to hold an inquest in the middle of the forest. Readers probably expect that the tape recording of the Morepork will identify the killer, and Marsh doesn't disappoint them, but whom it identifies comes as a surprise.

Of Marsh's six short stories published after she became a professional writer, three seem to me excellent: "Morepork," "Chapter and Verse," and the short-short "The Cupid Mirror." The others have their points, and only one, Marsh's very first, "Death on the Air," is disappointing. Why then did she say that she was not a "dab" at writing short stories? Part of the reason can be attributed to modesty—or as she put it, "I haven't a lot of self-confidence." She often felt the same way about her novels as she did about her shorter works. When the interviewer Stephen Merrick asked her whether she was haunted by a voice whispering "Next time they'll find you out," she replied, "All the time. I feel it about every book I write. I always believe it to be thoroughly bad" (27). Modesty and self-doubt, however, do not explain why Marsh wrote such a small number of short stories. I think that Margaret Lewis's comment, quoted at the beginning of this article, is correct--that Marsh did not structure a work of fiction in such a way that it could conveniently fit into a short story mold. Marsh said about constructing her novels: "Very often I begin to write about these people in their immediate situation with no more than the scantiest framework for a plot and its denouement" (28). She remarked in the Merrick interview, "I might write six pages of this sort of nonsense and I'll hope something will come out of it. Something always does, though it's usually quite different from anything I'd imagined." She went on to say that the opening scene was the hardest section to write of a detective novel (29). A short story, trying to tell its tale in just a few words, didn't allow Marsh the luxury of a leisurely introduction of characters who will work out their relationships and how the mystery will flow from their interactions. It must, moreover, have been difficult for Marsh to write knowing that the opening section of a short story is usually the most important. But she was above all a craftswoman; even if something were difficult for her, she would work at it and do it right. And her best short stories show what a fine writer she was, even in a form she did not like.

ENDNOTES

1. Margaret Lewis, *Ngaio Marsh, A Life* (London: Chatto & Windus, 1991), 242.
2. Kathryne Slate McDorman, *Ngaio Marsh* (Boston: Twayne, 1991).
3. Lewis, *Ngaio Marsh*, 107. In fairness I should point out that only a few of the short stories fit into Lewis's biographical theme, and except for "Morepork," they do not affect McDorman's emphasis on what she calls Marsh's "New Zealand roots and British branches."
4. Jacques Barzun and Wendell Hertig Taylor, *A Catalogue of Crime*, 2nd ed. (New York: Harper & Row, 1989), 649. They also mention (686) "Morepork" but comment only that it contains local color.
5. *Ellery Queen's Mystery Magazine*, August 1946, 5.
6. Ngaio Marsh, *Black Beech and Honeydew* (Boston: Little Brown, 1965), 204.
7. John Dickson Carr, introduction to *Maiden Murders*, Mystery Writers of America Anthology (New York: Harper & Brothers, 1952), xi.
8. Marsh, *Black Beech and Honeydew*, 204.
9. Lewis, *Ngaio Marsh*, 14, 37.
10. *The Collected Short Fiction of Ngaio Marsh*, ed. Douglas G. Greene, 2nd ed. (New York: International Polygonics, 1991), 242. Hereafter this book will be cited as *CSF*.

11. McDorman, *Ngaio Marsh*, 3.
12. Based on information in the files of Marsh's US agents, I wrote in the introduction to *CSF* that the story was published in 1939. The researches of Tony Medawar and information in the possession of her British agents date the publication December 1934. The first US publication was in *Ellery Queen's Mystery Magazine*, January 1948.
13. *CSF*, 42.
14. Ibid., 42, 56.
15. Ibid., 62.
16. Lewis, *Ngaio Marsh*, 107.
17. *CSF*, 95.
18. Ibid., 138.
19. *Argosy* (Britain), May 1969, 49.
20. Francis M. Nevins, Jr., review of *CSF* in *Mystery Scene* 25, March 1990, 57.
21. Letter from Ngaio Marsh to Douglas G. Greene, August 18, 1981.
22. Lewis, *Ngaio Marsh*, 222.
23. *CSF*, 142.
24. Ibid., 146.
25. Lewis, *Ngaio Marsh*, 83, 225-26. I am grateful to H. R. F. Keating for a copy of the Detection Club's membership list, which includes the date of Marsh's induction.
26. *CSF*, 147.
27. *Argosy*, May 1969, 44.
28. Ngaio Marsh, "Starting with People," *The Mystery and Detection Annual* (Beverly Hills: Donald Adams, 1973), 209.
29. *Argosy*, May 1969, 45-46.

"The Great and True Amphibian": The New Zealand/England Polarity in the Short Fiction of Ngaio Marsh

by Bruce Harding

In December 1950 Ngaio Marsh (OBE 1948), a fresh visitor to postwar Britain, gave an illustrated address to the Dominions and Colonies Section of The Royal Society of Arts in London. The High Commissioner for New Zealand, the Rt. Hon. W. J. Jordan (a Kiwi), welcomed Marsh "back to this Great Britain" (1)--despite the fact that she had been in the U. K. since July 1949, in time for the Penguin Books launch of "The Marsh Million" (100,000 copies of ten titles in paperback). Then he spoke of his keen anticipation in awaiting her reflections on "The Development of the Arts in New Zealand" as one who "stands high because of her abilities, among people in similar callings in Britain" (2). The singularity and quaintness of this tableau is worth remarking upon. Here one New Zealander (or colonial from a satellized nation) is welcoming another visitor from the periphery to address a gathering of people designated as member and/or supporters of the imperial dominions right in the heart of the Imperial Capital. Jordan's choice of diction is also revealing. Not only was Marsh acceptable as a cultural commentator when judged by the rigorous standards of the center of the *imperium*, but she would provide "another idea of that far-distant portion of our great Empire" (3)--New Zealand (or "Little England" as that nation has been teasingly dubbed). For her part, Marsh, the ardent devotee of the great spiritual partnership of Empire, did not disappoint her auditors, for even in discoursing upon the weakening of Imperial bonds--a "slowly fading nostalgia for the country of origin" (4), Ngaio--the ever-dutiful daughter of Albion--insisted that the true way forward for her nation's artists would be to graft from the robust stem of European "and, in particular, their British sources" (5). She thus echoed the sense of shared heritage expressed by Henry Parkes, the great architect of the Australian Federation, when he asserted, "The rich and comprehensive literature of England is ours as much as it is the possession of the British Islands" (6).

However, before assessing Marsh's emulation of British literary traditions and her fictional representation of her birth-land, it is worth asking something about how her own outlook was shaped by growing up in a strongly anglophone nation with a firmly colonial view of its place in the wider world which, in the years immediately following Queen Victoria's 60th Jubilee (1897), was still seen as co-extensive with the British Empire. For, apart from penning three short stories and five novels with significant New Zealand referents, Marsh exhibited a life-long interest in the production of a national culture, as reflected in her frequent tendency--adopting her idiom--to attitudinize for a largely British audience about the state of cultural progress in her homeland. The production of so much of this commentary seems to testify to an inner recognition that while she could not see the way clear to forge a robust post-colonial literary product herself, Marsh could at least see both the obstacles and opportunities ahead, and in a remarkably clear-sighted and helpful manner. And before I am roasted for the sin of reading contemporary obsessions back upon a child of her time, Marsh herself wrote in 1934 that she abandoned "a novel in a New Zealand setting" because she had begun "steaming off busily down the well-worn rails of the colonial novel" (7).

Marsh's own *modus operandi* was consonant with an idea of Edward Said: that we must pay greater attention to the place of narrative fiction in "the history and world of empire," for stories "become the method colonized people use to assert their own identity and the existence of their own history" (8). Marsh's peculiar genius was to mix the *tour d'horizon* (local vision) with the *tour du monde* which today we readily associate with an internationalist vision. Her best work also contained a subtle substratum of affectionate scrutiny of the British self-deception brought on by delusions of imperial grandeur. This is the place to cite Kathryne Slate McDorman's observation that Marsh's novels "are bursting with ideas about a wide range of topics, from the future of the British Commonwealth to the passing of Victorian-Edwardian manners and morals." McDorman correctly adds that Marsh

> explored a rather extensive sampling of Britons
> and New Zealanders to delineate not merely
> personal traits but national characteristics as
> well. As a social critic she deftly fileted Eng-
> land's class system, removing the skeleton still
> intact and exposing its shape and form to the
> last tiny bone (9).

Marsh's travel articles (written for the Associated Press in New Zealand between 1928-1931 while she was working hard in the Knightsbridge "Touch and Go" decorating shop) share Alan Mulgan's spirit of celebration of the *imperii centrum* (10) and convey its multiform delights and oddities to

her antipodal readership, for Marsh was always the archetypal
Antipodean sojourner: the person who could never give
absolutely final allegiance (cultural and spiritual) to either New
Zealand or England. In all of this we may argue that Ngaio
made the delightful discovery (even though it probably would
not have been a conscious one) that she could readily exist in
a state of social fluidity, with loyalties encompassing both
hemispheres, and inevitably recalling the description of Sir
Thomas Browne--in an altogether different context--of

> that great and true *amphibium*, whose nature is
> disposed to live not only like other creatures in
> divers elements, but in divided and distinguished
> worlds...(11)

II

        Reviewing Marsh's autobiography *Black Beech and
Honeydew* in 1966, the Australian novelist Kylie Tennant
posed the most pertinent question of Dame Ngaio's career:
"How does it come about that a female New Zealander should
glitter in the foremost ranks of popularity among the best
sellers of detective fiction?" (12) Tennant then pursued this
query by means of a particularly arresting comparison: "The
situation is at once piquant, ironic and charming, as though a
chieftaness from Celtic Britain should appear in Rome to
lecture on the benefits of law and the protection it gives to the
courtiers of Nero" (13).
        The first answer may be gleaned from Robin Winks,
who disagrees with the strictures of Edmund Wilson and even
Marshall McLuhan against "the artistic nullity of current
[1930's-40's] detective literature" (14). Winks provides the
central clue to its attraction as a form for Marsh: "It is moral

fiction" with "its fairytale childishness, its concern for detail, for order..." (15). And, of course, aside from its oft-discussed attraction for Ngaio as a shapely and economical genre, she practiced the classical--if impure--English variant, testing its very limits by occasionally shifting her locales right away from smog-bound London or what Margery Allingham called "the Oaken Heart" (16) of Christie's St. Mary Mead to places like New Zealand, yet all the while continuing to subscribe to the liberal enshrinement of the sovereign individual: the free, unified and autonomous selfhood celebrated in much of English culture. Marsh, while a self-declared "Whig to the Tories and Tory to the Whigs" (17), nonetheless upheld what Catherine Belsey skeptically defines as the "ideology of liberal humanism" which "assumes a world of non-contradictory (and therefore fundamentally unalterable) individuals whose unfettered consciousness is the origin of meaning, knowledge and action" (18).

The really critical point is that Marsh's socialization in Anglophile Christchurch inevitably led her to the kind of bifocal vision to which she herself alluded in giving her autobiography the alternative title of "Double Life" (19). In short, the answer to Tennant's question is inextricably tied up with the New Zealand-England dualism and its palpable effect on Ngaio's strong writerly ambitions which were in evidence from the times when she started dreaming about London and wanting to write: the very crucible of her emergent imagination was forged in an Anglocentric ambience. Marsh herself once spoke feelingly to me of the "agonizing and irreconcilable problem" of having loyalties (emotional and spiritual) divided between the hemispheres. While she deplored the "adolescent mentality" of many New Zealanders towards the arts and was indeed tempted, more than once, to live permanently in Britain after the death of her parents, she yet dearly loved the particular friends of her younger days and her own "blessed plot" of land in Valley Road, Cashmere (20). Marsh insisted that in leaving for the Home Country in 1928 she was not consciously escaping from local insularity or aesthetic philistinism:

> I was very young [she was actually almost 34]. I went principally because my great friends here [Helen and Tahu Rhodes] had gone and settled in England and they wanted me to go and live with them there. I had always wanted to go to England; I was born, almost, wanting to go to England, so all things came together for good for me. But I didn't think 'I am going to a better cultural environment' or anything like that (21).

This meeting with the Rhodes ménage (the Lampreys) was deeply formative and set the seal upon the influence of her father and of her London University-educated mentor, Miss Hughes, at St. Margaret's College, confirming as it did for Ngaio her then pre-existent certainty that wit, elegance, style and sophistication were more characteristic of the English. I firmly contend that this "Englishness" powerfully inflected all of Marsh's writing about her first homeland right until her last writing days; yet that restless emotional dialectic of allegiance worked both ways (a point often overlooked). Thus while it was easy for a reviewer to observe that "Miss Marsh writes in the richest English tradition," and to discern clear lines of derivation from Sayers and Allingham (22), when Samuel Marchbanks dubbed Marsh "the New Zealander upon whom the mantle of Dorothy L. Sayers appears to have fallen" and speculated about the probable origin of Roderick Alleyn, he unwittingly illustrated the perils of taking this one-sided, unproblematic view of Ngaio's Englandism too far. Marchbanks, logically enough, declared: "I cannot rid myself of a feeling that [Alleyn] was modelled, in her early books, very closely, upon Lord Peter Wimsey" (citing a deep emotional reticence amounting almost to bloodlessness) (23). When Marchbanks wrote of Wimsey and Alleyn as clear "creations of women," he referred to the preference of women of superior intelligence (Sayers and Marsh) for men who "are never the victims of their emotions, and [who] give expression to emotion only with the utmost reluctance and difficulty" (24).

While there is an affinity (which Marchbanks explained convincingly), there is another, more autobiographical, source worth pondering for the unexpected light which it throws upon Marsh's inner life. It seems more generous to surmise that Rory Alleyn was an idealized portrayal of Ned Bristed, the young man whom Ngaio described as "my great friend...perhaps a year my senior" (25). It is indeed teasing to relate that Marsh had Alleyn born in 1894 (a year before herself), and Margaret Lewis has written about Edward Bristed: "Although always very reticent about this relationship, Ngaio hinted in later years that there had been an understanding with Ned, and cherished a small ruby ring all her life for sentimental reasons" (26).

Patrick Cosgrove, noting Marsh's tendency to spend "most of her mature life between London and New Zealand, using each country as a bolt-hole," has discussed Ngaio's deeply romantic temperament in terms of her "highly romantic view of the English upper classes," adding that "it is hard to resist the idea that Alleyn is an idealized - and polished - version of Bristed" (27). If this speculation is correct, it becomes clear that Marsh based the two most intensely realized characters in her *oeuvre* upon two New Zealanders and imaginatively relocated them to London, so that Agatha Troy (an amalgam of herself) and Alleyn (Bristed) define an ideal marriage which had, in reality, been tragically foreclosed by the dreadful slaughter of the Great War.

Perhaps this accounts for Jessica Mann's comment--instancing this very issue of "affairs of the heart"--that Marsh "exemplifies in its most extreme form the reticence of the crime novelist"--one who "never grew irritated with her hero" and "never wrote anything which touched her emotions more deeply," leading Mann to the grim conclusion that Marsh's emotional reticence "has diminished the life of her novels" and will, more than anything, "determine whether they survive" (28). This has always struck me as an over-emphatic claim (especially to those who have learnt to decode Marsh's writings holistically and with an enhanced attention to their sub-text).

There are, however, even more complex leavenings underlying Marsh's New Zealand-England ambivalence. Earl Bargainnier has asserted: "Why Marsh has not more frequently used her native country" in her detective fictions "cannot be answered" (29). This is a useful spring-board to suggest some possible answers.

In her autobiography Marsh recalled that when the Rhodes family left for England in 1927 she had two ideas in her head: "one for a full-scale novel with a New Zealand background and one for a detective story as an exercise, or so I thought, in technique" (30). Marsh told me she later lost the typescript of the abortive New Zealand novel and stated that it was only the opportunity to make her long-awaited pilgrimage to England--which prevented her from continuing in this endeavor (31). However this assertion was written in 1964, and it clearly contradicts Marsh's version (written far closer to these events) penned in *The Press* a full thirty years earlier, in which she recalled that the opening chapters were promising enough:

"For a time it seemed to me that background
and figures worked well together, the one
growing up out of the other without too much
insistence on either. Then, after an interval, I
read what I had written and at once realised
that it would not do" (32).

Marsh admitted in a TV interview in 1966 that she

"would have liked to have written a serious
novel very much indeed, but I've always been
stopped by the feeling it might be just another
reasonably good long novel. I'm afraid *that* I
didn't want to do. I would rather write detective fiction efficiently than write a long novel
merely efficiently, if you see what I mean" (33).

As late as 1969 she stated that she would still like to write "a
serious novel with an early New Zealand background" in a
David Garnett, "choosey" vein (34). I would suggest that the
shapeliness of the detective form corresponded to Marsh's
love of good social form and, therefore, that she was, in all
probability, defeated by the comparative shapelessness of
New Zealand social experience. She told Edward Blishen in
1975 that the classical shape "attracted me very much indeed"
(35), and in 1978 Marsh expanded upon her "dread of writing
just another interminable novel": "I went all through the days
of those interminable American novels where the author
begins until he's got nothing more to say and then stops"
[instancing Allan Drury's *Advise and Consent*, Hervey Allen's
Anthony Adverse and Margaret Mitchell's *Gone with the
Wind*]. "It just goes on and on - there's no economy in the
writing at all. I didn't want to write like that: I didn't want to
turn out a New Zealand novel of immense length" (36).

Pressed further, Marsh admitted, "I'm not sure I would write it well enough to satisfy myself" (37). While Marsh had a self-described "horror of being pompous" about her novels, she was capable of spirited fighting talk in repudiation of cultural snobbery:

> "I'll defend them [detective novels] to the last
> ditch because I think you can write as well as
> you are able in that form, otherwise I wouldn't
> write them. My main aim is always to write as
> well as I can. That comes by a long way first,
> and the fact that they are cast in that form is
> secondary" (38).

We must ask why Ngaio felt so defensive. The main answer, alas, has a great deal to do with limited and imprisoning New Zealand attitudes: Ngaio's "eccentric" foray into what the local High Culturati condemned as mere "popular fiction" was barely tolerated and rarely venerated in the land of her birth.

In her autobiography Marsh had expanded upon the double insularity besetting her compatriots (39) with their odd mixture of complacency and uncertainty (40), but in 1934 she had judiciously observed, "Lack of aesthetic sympathy, though to be sure it flourishes here, loathsomely enough, is not peculiar to New Zealand" (41). In 1940 Marsh expanded upon her earlier observation that second- and third-generation writers were so "anxious to be 'New Zealand' at all costs that they overloaded their poems and short stories and novels with local colour, Maori words, and colonial slang" (42). This problem was still being discussed in Chapter 7.III of *Died in the Wool* (1944). Marsh described New Zealand as an adolescent nation, still in a transitional stage and thus very confused or too self-conscious in its imaginative writing. She insisted that soon the nation would be adult, and the reporter noted, "There was no criticism or condemnation implied in the theories [Marsh] had stated" (43). Yet as Carole Acheson has shrewdly observed, "In such a context Marsh's unashamedly middle-class, English, artistic background and outspoken comments on her country's shortcomings could hardly fail to arouse hostility" in an egalitarian and nationalistic climate (44).

Yet Marsh actually had embraced the necessity for cultural nationalism even though in the theatre she was an enthusiastic purveyor of the received intra-imperial and Anglocentric "Dominion culture" of her youth (as shown by her formation, in the Festival of Britain year of 1951, of The British Commonwealth Theatre Company). Graham Holderness writes very incisively about the political use made (from the Tudors onwards) of the Shakespeare myth of organic national unity, in which cultural power "was gradually and intentionally drawn, along with political power, towards the center..." (45). Applying this model to New Zealand in later years, and building upon her quest for a national theatre there, Ngaio spoke with clear approval of the 1972-75 Australian Whitlam Labor Government in terms of a nation "galvanized by a Prime Minister who not only valued cultural nationalism but was willing to provide funds to make it flourish" (46)--a statement which rather puts paid to Mervyn Thompson's charge that Ngaio "looked backwards to a charnel Empire/When new destiny lay just a dream ahead" (47).

III

If Ngaio had a cosmopolitan yet home-grown literary mentor, it was Katherine Mansfield (whose story "The Voyage" preceded Marsh's "The Figure Quoted" in O. N. Gillespie's pioneering collection of 1930, *New Zealand Short Stories*, which must inevitably have been a heady juxtaposition

for Ngaio, then living in London where the book appeared).
She recalled being introduced to Mansfield's work by her
mother who urged Ngaio to read Mansfield's carefully crafted
fictions. Marsh later asserted that these conveyed an
"extremely accurate" picture of what it felt like to grow up
amidst a genteel family in New Zealand in the early 1900's
(48). Marsh clearly saw in Mansfield an excellent model for
an emergent national literature: "because she isn't writing her
boots off to create local colour she remains one of the most
successful of our writers to do precisely that thing" (49). In
1945 Marsh praised Mansfield for her "style" (the single
criterion of value by which Marsh most wanted her own work
to be judged), as a peerless exemplar of "how a short story
may be ripened and nursed before it is plucked, and how in
writing, a nuance may echo an emotion and a cadence
faithfully give out the inward breath of an idea" (50). This
recurring appeal to Mansfield as a model has much to do with
answering Kylie Tennant's question (i.e. showing why Marsh's
work could be described by Sutherland Scott as an instance of
"British mystery-making at its most typical" [51]) and also in
explaining why she never managed to write that novel about
the pioneering days of New Zealand and why so much of
Marsh's writing about her homeland suffers slightly from a
sense of occlusion (52).

Her vision of the Commonwealth bond has been
capably delineated by Kathryne Slate McDorman (53) and
could as easily have emerged from the office of H. M. the
Queen in Buckingham Palace as from Marton Cottage,
Cashmere. This may well have been what Margaret Lewis
meant when, discussing Ngaio's syndicated travel articles, she
defined Marsh's attitude as being "close to the hazy desires" of
her youthful and derivative plays, *The Moon Princess* and
Little Housebound (54). As Lewis bluntly asserts: "What
made Ngaio unusual was that she was a born New Zealander,

and her image of 'home' was entirely fictitious" (55). David
Hall once explored this point a little more generously:

> Her own family had its feet firmly planted on
> the earth of this time and place, but its head
> was enveloped still in a nostalgic cloud, neither
> long nor white, but fleecy, rose-tinted English.
> How many New Zealand families judge life
> by standards drawn from another country?
> Christchurch-born, private-school educated...
> and with a 'public school' father, she had a
> more natural attraction to 'Home' (not a New
> Zealander's adventure, in Alan Mulgan's phrase,
> but rather a birthright) than most; it is sur-
> prising only that she waited so long to go to
> England (56).

Ngaio Marsh ·was born into the conservative and
socially compact little community of late Victorian
Christchurch. Her parents--British born Henry Marsh and
colonial Rose Seager--were married on 24 April 1894 and
their only child, Edith Ngaio, was born on 23 April 1895 and
baptized into the colony's prestige faith, the Anglican
communion, on 16 June 1895 (57). Ngaio's date of birth was,
appropriately enough, St. George's Day as well as the
legendary birthdate of William Shakespeare. The birth of this
child in the closing years of Queen Victoria's reign and her
growing up in the twilight--albeit a transferred one--of the
Edwardian era were to prove crucial in shaping the prevailing
temper and tone of her outlook, particularly when Marsh set
out to experiment with writing as a young woman.
    The Marshes may have been poor, but they still
managed to employ a maid (and, later, a governess), and it is
apparent that Ngaio Marsh's upbringing reflected a somewhat

uneasy compromise between English and pioneering,
mainstream New Zealand values, to the virtual exclusion of
the latter. This is best instanced in the attitude of her mother,
a local, who yet "doggedly determined that I should not
acquire the accent" (58). While Henry Marsh "talked an awful
lot about England and about London" (he was, in effect, a
Londoner), Mrs. Marsh "had the same feeling about it
although she had never been there" (59). It is surely clear how
the die for Ngaio's New Zealand ambivalence was cast.

Dame Ngaio described her early fixation on England
as "very curious"; she recalled that her early childish dreams
of London were not unlike the reality she later experienced,
and she was particularly fascinated by a silent, jerky
travelogue film called "Living London" which her family went
to see at least twice (60).

Marsh's writing career began when, as a promising
student at the Canterbury College School of Art, she met
socially the editor of *The Sun* evening newspaper, Edward
Huie, who, enjoying her spoken account of an eventful rail
journey from Westland back to the city, asked her to write it
up. Once "The Night Train from Grey" was published, Ngaio
was surprised to find that "it was rather popular" with his
readers (61). So began her "first venture in professional
writing" (62) and a sporadic but productive association with
this progressive newspaper between 1918 and 1925, by her
own account. In total Ngaio had about six short stories
eventually published in *The Sun*, and her obvious facility for
strong journalistic writing led to a stint as a stand-in Lady-
Editor (social columnist) for a month around March 1920.

It is really important to stress how fortunate Ngaio
was in gaining this experience, for Huie (an Australian)
created *The Sun* in February 1914, modelling it on London's
Daily Mail and livening up Christchurch's pedestrian
journalistic scene by creating (in the words of pioneering

author Robin Hyde) "the one and only daily [in New Zealand] to pay any serious attention to literary work - poems, short stories, articles - garnered in from the stores of New Zealand writers" (63). As P. A. Lawlor noted in 1935, *The Sun* "was a newspaper of originality" edited by "one of the finest editor-managers we have known" (Huie) and "the pivot of its enterprise, its literary staff, was unequalled in the history of journalism" in New Zealand (64).

The Anglophile inflection to her whole *oeuvre* may be traced clearly in the two of those six *Sun* stories which have come to light. Ngaio thought she penned "Moonshine" at the age of nineteen, but it is likely to have followed "The Night Train from Grey" which Lewis dates from 1919 (65). Marsh motifs abound in "Moonshine," amply reflecting the perspective of a young woman raised in a colony whose Founders aimed, principally, "to make their Settlement differ from others in being more, than in any previous case, *an extension of England with regard to the more refined attributes of civilization*" (66). This fiction uses the Marsh punning title that became known as her hallmark. Father Christmas is not only a northern myth, but his youthful and soon to be disillusioned Antipodean acolyte, Janey, waits for him in an open balcony verandah in the moonlight of a summer evening while listening to the cabbage tree (*tinui*) leaves "lisping together very slightly" (p. 21) (67). The setting is demonstrably colonial Christchurch (local references to the dim blue mountains, "the flat," the gully of Valley Road, Dyers Pass Road, which was where Ngaio and Rose went across open grasslands to attend service at St. Augustine's Anglican Church--all attest this); but the sensibility informing the text is as thoroughly English as that to be found in early stories by Mansfield (e.g., "Enna Blake," "A Happy Christmas Eve," and "Almost a Tragedy" (68).

The story is delightful in its suggestions of Marsh family life with the young Janey erupting into a flood of passionate emotions, as Marsh used to as a young woman. Her father is clearly·modelled upon Henry Marsh in his rationalistic rantings about carol singers (pp. 23-24), and in the little girl Ngaio even parodies her own atrocious youthful spelling. The evocation of deep affectional ties with parents completes the authenticity of the portrayal and makes "Moonshine" a satisfying statement about a young and intelligent child (an empiricist at heart) growing up and, for that emotional richness, makes it a far more important text than a bolder exercise in craftsmanship like "Morepork" could ever be. It is, like the best of Marsh's fiction, heavily charged with an autobiographical resonance.

The second known *Sun* story, "The Figure Quoted" (1927) (69), strikes a posturing note and calls to mind the adage of an early Canterbury University English professor, Frederick Sinclaire (1881-1954), who wrote in 1935 that to be "very much at home" is to "overcome the first and perhaps the most serious obstacle to the development of a genuine culture" (70). For the *socius* of "The Figure Quoted" is as likely to be London as it is to be anywhere else, but in 1927 Ngaio was aged thirty-two and had still never left New Zealand's shores. "The Figure Quoted" is a wonderfully ironic comic evocation of what Freud called "the return of the repressed," as it sends up a crudely pragmatic small business operator and his gathering incomprehension as "The whole of his everyday business had become pagan and improper" (p. 216), demolishing the quotidian and puritan stuffiness of a life enslaved to routine. There are two comic thrusts which may suggest a New Zealand setting: the commercial equivalence of a meat-dish and the works of Lord Byron on the sales list (p. 212) and the auctioneer's habitual mistrust of imagination

("It was a quality of his mind in which he was not interested" [p. 212]).

Years later, in *Colour Scheme* (1943), Marsh offered this slightly romantic and almost political observation about the relationship between the *tangata whenua* (indegenes) and Papatuanuku (Mother Earth): "White men move across the surface of New Zealand, but the Maori people are of its essence, tranquil or disturbed as the trees and lakes must be, and as much a member of the earth as they" (71). In moments like these Ngaio threw off that partially occluded vision under which she clearly labored in works such as "The Figure Quoted." For despite its formal excellence, its lexical playfulness, and abundant evidence of craft, it is the work of a person inured to the belief that Australasians "were borrowers, parasites feeding on food produced abroad," as Manning Clark put it (72). Clark added a useful gloss on Marsh's botanical metaphor, writing that in his youth Australia "was a tree kept alive by feeding off the giants in the forests of European culture" (73).

To return to the concept of Marsh's occasional referential occlusiveness, one must note that the anthologist O. N. Gillespie discoursed at some length as to why many of the stories offered in his volume "may prove disappointing" because, "particularly by contrast with those from Australia, [they] lack any national outlook or distinctive atmosphere" (74). Gillespie cited as a critical factor the unified purpose of New Zealanders "to refashion in these islands the homeland they had left" (75). Another reason why "The Figure Quoted" does not (in Gillespie's terms) "relate to New Zealand" (76) is that at this time Ngaio was probably still impressed and influenced by the short stories of E. M. Forster and Walter de la Mare and anxious to avoid producing sterile exercises in what she called "pseudo-colonial romanticism" (77). Or the explanation for the echoing emptiness of "The Figure Quoted"

may simply lie in the influence of derivative English plays
which Ngaio had been acting in and/or directing, along with
pantomimes and Anglocentric charity shows in the 'twenties,
such as *The Sleeping Beauty* for Unlimited Charities.
    As early as 1934 Marsh had written that "the landscape
can be felt only through the spiritual and mental experiences
of human beings" and that if these are successfully realized and
integrated, "it may be that the shapes of mountains and rivers
will appear, not as so many theatrical properties, but
inevitably, so that the story could have unfolded in no other
setting" (78). Yet in 1950 she was unhelpfully painting a
portrait of melancholy and brooding New Zealand provincials
marooned in "a lonely group of islands in a great waste of
waters down at the bottom of the world," whose inhabitants
"are almost morbidly conscious of their isolation" (79).
Marsh's charge that living (in Allen Curnow's terms) "Not in
Narrow Seas" (80) separates the Kiwis "not only physically
from our mother country and our nearest neighbour but in all
matters of the mind and spirit" (81) lays her wide open to the
assertion that she was seriously lacking what John Pocock has
thoughtfully termed "a *tangata whenua* humanism"--a means
of poetic appropriation involving "dreaming or imagining one's
way into a relationship with the environment" (82) which one
can see to good effect in her youthful poem "Bushman's Song"
(83) and in her later description of "the violent landscape" of
her birthland, with "the uncompromising clarity where blue
screams blueness and vegetation lies in clots of wicked green
on knife-edged mountains..." (84). If we ally Marsh's
strictures against indigenous writers with a facility for "setting
down the local scene and a complete failure to find any kind
of universal conclusion from it" (85) (as a species of empty
reportage) with her own recognition of the West Coast as a
source of the authentic "mother lode" for the full-dress New
Zealand novel, we are confronted once again with Ngaio's

own inner insecurities and anxieties about doing justice to this unyielding landscape--and all of that, I contend, is intimately connected to her too strong and inhibiting sense of the cultural dues owed by one homeland (the peripheral) to another ("Home"). For in that RSA lecture of 1950, Ngaio virtually fawned in her insistence that her generation of writers was inevitably bound "by our history and heritage, to a tradition some of us were not altogether willing to acknowledge," instancing D'Arcy Cresswell's archaic *Poet's Progress* (1930) for showing "us how admirably the continuity of [British] tradition can sustain a writer who concerns himself with the New Zealand scene" (86).

However, Ngaio looked ahead for "a penetrating and aesthetically satisfying novel born of [the] formidable" Westland landscape (87). But even in Marsh's best prose a slightly quaint and curiously detached commentary-description prevails in the nineteenth-century tradition of travelogue writing. There are some wondrous exceptions to this, especially in *Vintage Murder* (1937), *Colour Scheme* (1943), and *Died in the Wool* (1944), which I have previously discussed (88). These three novels were written immediately before and during World War II, a time when Marsh looked long and hard at her homeland, threatened as it was after the fall of Singapore as the Japanese made their way down into their "Greater Co-Prosperity Sphere." Forty years later, one may say that the genuine New Zealand novel has at last emerged. There is a much higher concentration and level of emotional response to, and celebration of, New Zealand land and seascapes in Book II (The Sea Round) of Keri Hulme's *the bone people*, at Kerewin Holmes's arrival at Moerangi. The author's evident self-investment in the land is revealed there (pp. 162-66)--culminating in Kerewin's litany: "o land, you're too deep in my heart and mind. o sea, you're the blood of me"

(p. 166) (89). Such passages sharpen the distinction between colonized and truly post-colonial prose.

I should like to demonstrate this contrast using Marsh's justly-praised final short story, "Morepork" (1978) (90). Ngaio's final three novels with New Zealand settings are very important but in "Morepork," *Photo Finish* (1980), and *Light Thickens* (1982) the demands of locale (or of New Zealand character) have been strictly subordinated to the dominant exigencies of the form.

"Morepork" is, like "Moonshine," to some extent what Eliot called an "objective correlative" for Marsh, for it is reminiscent of Marsh's writings about her own summer holidays in the Glentui area (Oxford, North Canterbury) where she and a friend slept out under the trees. It is a finely constructed tale with a richly textured sense of locale. Yet here again Ngaio cannot do without an Englishman in the person of Miles Curtis-Vane, the one Briton in a party of Kiwi deer-stalkers whose clothes, although "well-worn, had a distinctive look which they would have retained if they had been rags" (p. 166). Curtis-Vane stands a breed apart from the sturdy New Zealanders. When the leading lady (Susan Bridgeman) arrives, having learned that her estranged husband has died after falling off a jerry-built bridge into the treacherous Wainui (a snow-fed river), like her son Clive she instinctively settles for Curtis-Vane to render general gratitude to the group who recovered the body (p. 171). At the end of this ingenious plot we learn that the Maori regarded the morepork not merely--in Arthur Vogan's words--as the "night jar of Australasia" (91) but, in the recorded words of the deceased, as "a harbinger of death" (p. 183). The murderers over-reach themselves and the solution to the mystery of Caley's demise hinges on a piece of technical apparatus. These villains spoke of their murderous intent in the bush away from the campers, but not away from the range of Caley Bridgeman's highly sensitive parabolic microphone. A prerequisite in the writing of "Morepork" was Julian Symons's insistence that all stories in the anthology had to in some way involve a trial by jury (makeshift or otherwise). Marsh handled this requirement with typical resourcefulness, yet this situation does force out the most tedious passages in the text and of necessity creates another of many occasions in Marsh's *oeuvre* for unequipped colonials to defer to an Englishman: Gosse leaves it for Curtis-Vane to establish the terms of reference and to run the *plein-air* "inquiry" (pp. 177-78). "Morepork" is thus, for all its excellence, finally a piece of plot-driven machinery which hums along efficiently. However, Marsh was confined by the Symons requirement (the Center quite unwittingly confining the presentation of the exotic margin), even though I doubt that she was at all aware of the fact.

The quality of the best descriptive prose in "Morepork" and *Photo Finish* leads one to regret, very deeply, that Ngaio never left the somewhat shallow water allowed to her by the genre of detective fiction to write more open-heartedly, in a novel, of the love she bore for her native land. For, as McDorman rightly emphasized, Marsh's commitment to excellence, "be it in popular fiction or classical theater, argues persuasively for recognizing her for what she was, a woman of letters" (92). And in fact, in 1962 Ngaio received the first Honorary Doctor of Literature degree from the University of Canterbury, the citation justly celebrating her "services to the arts" and noting that "we can admire--and envy--her diligent application, her craftsmanship and [her] inventiveness...as one who has done so much for the literary reputation of our nation..." (93).

Dame Ngaio lies buried in the churchyard of the Anglican Church of the Holy Innocents on the Mount Peel

Station (South Canterbury), in the foothills of the Southern
Alps she loved so passionately.   There can be no more fitting
means of closing these reflections about Ngaio's ultimate
bondedness to the landscape of her nativity than to take
respectful leave of her with these lines from a poem by Arnold
Wall:

> But I camp no more in the beech-wooded valleys,
> No more shall I sleep in the roar of the river,
> Or wander alone in the cool shady valleys,
> For my feet have come down to the lowlands
>   forever (94).

ENDNOTES

1. W. J. Jordan introducing Marsh, "The Development of
   the Arts in New Zealand," *Journal of the Royal
   Society of Arts*, Vol. XCIX, No. 4840 (9 February
   1951), 247.
2. Jordan, 247.
3. Jordan, 247.
4. Marsh quoted by Jordan, 248.
5. Marsh quoted by Jordan, 248.
6. Parkes, quoted by Stephen Alomes, *A Nation at Last?
   The Changing Character of Australian Nationalism
   1880-1988* (North Ryde, NSW: Angus & Robertson,
   1988), 31.
7. Ngaio Marsh, "The Background," *The Press*
   [Christchurch], 22 December 1934.
8. Edward W. Said, *Culture and Imperialism* (London:
   Chatto & Windus, 1993), xiii.

9. Kathryne Slate McDorman, *Ngaio Marsh*, Twayne's English Authors Series 481 (Boston, MA: Twayne Publishers/G. K. Hall, 1991), 140.

10. Alan Mulgan, *Home: A Colonial's Adventure* (London: Longmans Green & Co., 1927; new ed. 1929).

11. Sir Thomas Browne, *Religio Medici* (London: Andrew Cooke, 1643); rpt. & ed. Henry Gardiner (London: William Pickering, 177, Piccadilly, 1845), 89.

12. Kylie Tennant, "Ngaio Marsh and her detective," *The Sydney Morning Herald* (Weekend Magazine & Book Reviews), 9 July 1966, 17.

13. Ibid.

14. H. M. McLuhan, "Footprints in the Sands of Crime," *The Sewanee Review*, Vol. LIV: 4 (Autumn 1946), 620.

15. Robin W. Winks, "Introduction" to *Detective Fiction: A Collection of Critical Essays* (Englewood Cliffs, New Jersey: Prentice-Hall, 1980) 9-10.

16. Margery Allingham, *The Oaken Heart* (London: Michael Joseph, 1941).

17. Marsh to Harding, 21 January 1979.

18. C. Belsey, *Critical Practice* (London: Methuen, 1980), 67.

19. Cf. the holographic MS. of *Black Beech and Honeydew* (other titles being "It So Happened" and "It So Fell Out") in The Twentieth Century Authors Collection, Mugar Memorial Library (Boston University Libraries, Boston, Massachusetts).

20. Marsh to Harding, 21 January 1979.

21. Marsh to Harding, 23 June 1978.

22. "Latest Post-Mortems," *The Bulletin* [Philadelphia], 1947 (no author or exact publication date specified) in Marsh's clipping book.

23. Samuel Marchbanks, "The Great Detective," *The Peterborough Examiner* [Ontario, Canada], 4 June 1947, n.p.
24. Ibid.
25. Ngaio Marsh, *Black Beech and Honeydew* (London: Collins, 1966), 31.
26. Margaret Lewis, *Ngaio Marsh: A Life* (London: Chatto & Windus, 1991), 21.
27. Patrick Cosgrave, "Red Herrings and ruby rings," *The Independent*, 4 May 1991.
28. Jessica Mann, *Deadlier Than the Male: An Investigation into Feminine Crime Writing* (Newton Abbot, Devon: David & Charles, 1981), 221, 224, 233.
29. Earl F. Bargainnier, "Ngaio Marsh" in *Ten Women of Mystery* (Bowling Green, Ohio: Bowling Green University Popular Press, 1981), 95.
30. Marsh, *Black Beech and Honeydew*, 171.
31. Ibid., 172 cf. also 217.
32. Ngaio Marsh, "The Background," *The Press*, 22 December 1934.
33. Ngaio Marsh, "Three Several Quests," NZBC TV, 1966, [Interviewer: Alex McDowell].
34. Marsh to Stephen Merrick, *Argosy*, Vol. XXX:5 (May 1969), 48.
35. Marsh to Blishen, (BBC Radio, 1975): rebroadcast YA network (Radio New Zealand), 26 June 1982.
36. Marsh to Harding, 7 April 1978.
37. Ibid.
38. Marsh to Harding, 23 June 1978.
39. This is that classic passage: "We are often told by English people how very English New Zealand is, their intention being complimentary. I think that this pronouncement may be true but not altogether in the

intended sense. We are, I venture, more like the
English of our pioneers' time than those of our own.
We are doubly insular. We come from a group of
islands at the top of the world and we have settled on a
group comparable in size but infinitely more isolated, at
the bottom of it. We are overwhelmingly of English,
Scottish, Welsh and Irish stock and it seemed to me,
when I came back after five years, that we had turned
in on our origins. You might say, I thought, that if you
put a selection of people from the British Isles into
antipodean cold-storage for a century and a half and
then opened the door: we are what would emerge."
(Black Beech and Honeydew [1966], 224).

40. Marsh wrote that, returning from Europe in November
1932, she thought "how complacent we [Kiwis] are and
yet how uncertain of ourselves! Why do the young
ones say so often and so proudly that they suppose
New Zealand seems crude and then, if you agree:
'Well, in some ways, perhaps,' why do they look so
furious? I had forgotten what we are like, I thought.
We really are rum. Or so it seemed to me when I
returned." (Ibid., 225).

41. Marsh, "The Background," *The Press* [Christchurch],
22 December 1934.

42. Ibid.

43. "She Took to Crime for a Joke," *NZ Listener*, 21
March 1940, 24 [author unknown].

44. Carole Acheson, "Cultural Ambivalence: Ngaio
Marsh's New Zealand Detective Fiction," *Journal of
Popular Culture*, Vol. 19:2 (Fall 1985), 161-62.

45. Cf. Graham Holderness, *Shakespeare's History*
(Dublin: Gill & Macmillan/New York: St. Martin's
Press, 1985), 159. Holderness's discussion of this
ideological use of Shakespeare in wartime Britain

(178-95) is particularly acute, and this was a process which Marsh closely observed and then followed with her legendary student productions of Shakespeare at the University of Canterbury (1943-67) and then in choosing to open the new theatre of the Christchurch Town Hall with *Henry V* (the culmination of the Tudor myth) in 1972. Margaret Lewis discusses the "painful failure" of the British Commonwealth Theatre Company and Ngaio's interest in the formation of a National Theatre in New Zealand in *Ngaio Marsh: A Life*, 137-40; 148-49.

46. Marsh, quoted by Elizabeth Riddell, "One wet afternoon" (Review), *The Bulletin* [Sydney], 4 June 1991, 106.

47. Mervyn Thompson, "On the Death of Ngaio Marsh," *Landfall* 144 (Vol. 36:4) [December 1982], 445.

48. Marsh to Harding, 7 January 1979.

49. Marsh, quoted by Margaret Lewis, 53.

50. Ibid., 188-89.

51. Cf. Sutherland Scott's comment: "Although Miss Marsh is a New Zealander, she can, by every count, be grouped with the home product" (*Blood in Their Ink: The March of the Modern Mystery Novel* (London: Stanley Paul & Co., 1953), 66.

52. Marsh's treatment of New Zealand in her published fiction has been discussed illuminatingly by Carole Acheson in "Cultural Ambivalence: Ngaio Marsh 's New Zealand Detective Fiction," *Journal of Popular Culture*, Vol. 19:2 (Fall 1985), 159-74 and by Bruce Harding in "The New Zealand Stories of Ngaio Marsh," *Landfall* 144 (Vol. 36:4 [December 1982]), 447-60. Both of these essays, written by New Zealanders residing in Christchurch, were reprinted in abridged form in *Contemporary Literary Criticism*,

Vol. 53 (Detroit, Michigan: Gale Research Inc., 1989), 254-60.

53. McDorman, *Ngaio Marsh*, Chapter Two: "Images of Commonwealth," 20-45.

54. Lewis, *Ngaio Marsh: A Life*, 41.

55. Ibid., 40.

56. David Hall, "Grease Paint Before Corpses," *NZ Listener*, Vol. 54:1387 (6 May 1966), 20.

57. St. Michael's Anglican Church Transcript of Marriages, 1879-1912 (entry 150C) and Transcript of Baptisms, 1884-1902 (entry 5819).

58. Marsh, *Black Beech and Honeydew*, 18.

59. Marsh, "Three Several Quests" (1966).

60. Marsh to Harding, 21 June 1979.

61. Marsh to Harding, 7 April 1978.

62. Marsh, *Black Beech and Honeydew*, 118: "I began writing for the long-defunct *Sun* soon after I left school - short stories, articles, verse. None of which I have preserved. I was at that time a great admirer of Walter de la Mare and the short stories of E. M. Forster. There was one short story - a fantasy which I'm sorry I didn't keep - which reflected their influence." (Written communication to Harding, June-July 1978). Dame Ngaio referred to this "bastard offspring" of Forster's "Celestial Omnibus" in *Black Beech and Honeydew*, 121; 171-72.

63. Robin Hyde, *Journalese* (Auckland: National Printing Co., 1934), 191.

64. Pat Lawlor, *Confessions of a Journalist* (Auckland: Whitcombe & Tombs, 1935), 155, 153.

65. Lewis, *Ngaio Marsh: A Life*, 23.

66. *Canterbury Settlement; with some account of the sources from which full information may be derived.* Published for the Society of Canterbury Colonists by

J. W. Parker, West Strand (London), n.d. but prob. 1848/49.

67. All references to "Moonshine" (which was probably first published in *The Sun*) are from *Yours and Mine: Stories by Young New Zealanders*, ed. Warwick Lawrence (New Plymouth: Thomas Avery & Sons, 1936).

68. "Enna Blake" and "A Happy Christmas Eve" have been republished in *The Stories of Katherine Mansfield: Definitive Edition,* ed. Antony Alpers (Auckland: Oxford University Press, 1984), 1-3. "Almost a Tragedy: The Cars on Lambton Quay" was published in the *New Zealand Listener*, 11 July 1987, 25.

69. First published in *The Sun*, December 1927, the story was reprinted in *New Zealand Short Stories*, ed. O. N. Gillespie (London: J. M. Dent & Sons, 1930; rpt. 1932), 209-18. (My references are to this text.) The story has been republished for North American readers in *The Collected Short Fiction of Ngaio Marsh*, ed. Douglas G. Greene (New York: International Polygonics Ltd., 1989; rpt. 1991), 241-49.

70. Frederick Sinclaire, "Notes by the Way," *Tomorrow*, Vol. 1:40 (31 July 1935), 7.

71. Ngaio Marsh, *Colour Scheme* (London: Collins/ Fontana, 1969), 24.

72. Manning Clark, *The Quest for Grace* (Ringwood, Victoria: Viking/Penguin Books Australia, 1990; rpt. 1991), 20.

73. Clark, 39.

74. O. N. Gillespie, "Preface" to *New Zealand Short Stories*, v.

75. Ibid.

76. Ibid., vii

77. Marsh, *Black Beech and Honeydew*, 121.

78. Marsh, "The Background," *The Press*, 22 December 1934.
79. Ngaio Marsh, "The Development of the Arts in New Zealand," 247.
80. Allen Curnow, *Not in Narrow Seas: Poems with Prose* (Christchurch: Caxton Press, 1939); rpt. in *Allen Curnow: Selected Poems* (Auckland: Penguin Books NZ Ltd., 1982), 1-25.
81. Marsh, "The Development of the Arts in New Zealand," 247.
82. J. G. A. Pocock, "*Tangua whenua* and Enlightenment Anthropology;" paper read to The New Zealand Historical Association Conference, University of Canterbury (11-15 May 1991), 29.
83. As a school girl Ngaio published in *St. Margaret's College Magazine* a Kiplingesque poem, "The Bushman's Song," celebrating the Westland.
84. Ngaio Marsh, "Achievement in Fine Arts," *The Times* (Supplement on NZ), 6 February 1963, vi.
85. Marsh, "The Development of the Arts in New Zealand," 253.
86. Ibid., 252, 253.
87. Marsh, *Black Beech and Honeydew*, 121.
88. Cf. my essay, "The New Zealand Stories of Ngaio Marsh," *Landfall* 144 (December 1982), 447-60, and "Wrestling with Caliban: Patterns of the Bi-Racial Encounter in Ngaio Marsh's *Colour Scheme* (1943)," and Alan Duff's "Once There Were Warriors" (1990), *Australian and New Zealand Studies in Canada*, No. 8 (December 1992), 136-55.
89. Keri Hulme, *the bone people* (Wellington: Spiral Collective, 1984; rpt. Baton Rouge, LA: Louisiana State University Press, 1985).

90. My reference has been to "Morepork" in *Verdict of Thirteen: A Detection Club Anthology,* ed. Julian Symons (London: Faber & Faber, 1979), 161-84. This anthology was first published by Harper and Row (New York) in 1978 as a Joan Kahn Book and "Morepork" has been re-published by International Polygonics and edited by Douglas G. Greene, *The Collected Short Fiction of Ngaio Marsh,* 147-74.
91. Arthur Vogan, *The Black Police* (London: Hutchinson, 1890), 88.
92. McDorman, *Ngaio Marsh,* 145.
93. "Recipients 'Bring Honour to University'," *The Christchurch Star,* 31 October 1962.
94. Arnold Wall, "The Old Botanist's Farewell to the Southern Alps" (1923); quoted by N. A. R. Barrer, *The Misty Isle* (Christchurch: Whitcombe & Tombs, 1966), 154.

Appendixes

A Chronology of Plays
Directed by Ngaio Marsh

Except where indicated otherwise, all productions are in Christchurch. Where known, the date of the first performance is given.

09 Sept 1913   *The Moon Princess* by Ngaio Marsh. At the St Michael's School Hall. Marsh assisted Miss Helen Burton, who directed the production.

1922   *Little Housebound* by Ngaio Marsh. Toured with two other plays to Hastings and Havelock North.

26 May 1924   *Bluebell in Fairyland.* For Unlimited Charities at the Theatre Royal. Marsh took over the rehearsals in the final weeks.

18 July 1925   *The Sleeping Beauty.* For Unlimited Charities at the Theatre Royal.

12 June 1926   *Cinderella* by Ngaio Marsh. For Unlimited Charities at the Theatre Royal. Marsh assisted the director, Mrs J. Hulme.

21 Sept 1938   *A Man's House* by John Drinkwater. For
                  the Dunedin Repertory Society at His
                  Majesty's Theatre, Dunedin.

23 Nov 1938   *The Late Christopher Bean* by Emlyn
                  Williams. For the Dunedin Repertory
                  Society at His Majesty's Theatre,
                  Dunedin.

29 March 1939   *The Anatomist* by James Bridie. For
                  the Dunedin Repertory Society at His
                  Majesty's Theatre, Dunedin.

1940   *The Last Hour.* For the Ashburton
                  Repertory Society at the Radiant
                  Hall, Ashburton.

31 July 1941   *Outward Bound* by Sutton Vane. For
                  the Canterbury University College
                  Drama Society at the Little Theatre.

03 Nov 1941   *The Soul of Nicholas Snyders.* For
                  the Ashburton Repertory Society at
                  the Radiant Hall, Ashburton.

Aug 1942   *Blithe Spirit* by Noel Coward. For
                  the Canterbury Repertory Theatre
                  Society at the Radiant Hall.

1942   *Blithe Spirit* by Coward. For the
                  Wellington Repertory Theatre,
                  Wellington.

1943	*The Corn Is Green* by Emlyn Williams. For the Wellington Repertory Theatre Society, Wellington.
02 Aug 1943	*Hamlet* by William Shakespeare. For the Canterbury University College Drama Society at the Little Theatre.
27 Nov 1943	*Hamlet.* (August production revived for a season at the Little Theatre.)
July 1944	*Othello* by Shakespeare. For the Canterbury University College Drama Society at the Little Theatre.
Oct 1944	*Distant Point* by Alexander Afinogenev. For the Canterbury Repertory Theatre Society at the Radiant Hall.

Tour of revived productions of *Othello* and *Hamlet* under the aegis of D.D. O'Connor:

17 Dec 1944	Town Hall Concert Chamber, Dunedin.
14 Jan 1945	His Majesty's Theatre, Auckland.
Jan 1945	Town Hall Concert Chamber, Wellington.
10 Feb 1945	Radiant Hall, Christchurch
26 July 1945	*A Midsummer Night's Dream* by Shakespeare. For the Canterbury University College Drama Society at the Radiant Hall.

08 Dec 1945   *King Henry V* by Shakespeare. For the
                 Canterbury University College
                 Drama Society at the Little Theatre.

14 April 1946   *What Say They?* For the Canterbury
                 University College Drama Society at
                 the Little Theatre. Marsh assisted
                 with this production.

20 July 1946   *Macbeth* by Shakespeare. For the
                 Canterbury University College
                 Drama Society at the Radiant Hall.

Sept 1947   *The Anatomist* by James Bridie. For
                 the Canterbury Repertory Theatre
                 Society at the Radiant Hall.

27 Sept 1948   Act One of *Six Characters in Search
                 of an Author* by Luigi Pirandello.
                 For the Canterbury University
                 College Drama Society in honour of
                 the visit of the Old Vic Company.
                 Private performance.

Tour of revived productions of *Six Characters in Search of
an Author* and *Othello* to Australia under the aegis of D.D.
O' Connor:

Jan 1949   Conservatorium, Sydney.

31 Jan 1949   Albert Hall, Canberra.

05 Feb 1949   Union Theatre, Melbourne.

Jan 1950   *Six Characters in Search of an Author*
                  by Pirandello. At the Embassy
                  Theatre, London.

1951   Tour of *The Devil's Disciple* by G.B.
                  Shaw, *Twelfth Night* by Shakespeare
                  and *Six Characters in Search of an
                  Author* by Pirandello to Australia and
                  New Zealand; by the British
                  Commonwealth Theatre Company
                  which Marsh founded.

29 Nov 1952   *A Sleep of Prisoners* by Christopher Fry.
                  For the Canterbury University
                  College Drama Society at the
                  Repertory Theatre (formerly the
                  Radiant Hall).

25 July 1953   *Julius Caesar* by Shakespeare. For the
                  Canterbury University College
                  Drama Society in the Great Hall,
                  Canterbury University College.

23 Aug 1956   *King Lear* by Shakespeare. For the
                  Canterbury University College
                  Drama Society at the Civic Theatre.

19 July 1957   *King Henry V* by Shakespeare. For the
                  Canterbury University College
                  Drama Society at the Civic Theatre.

11 July 1958   *Hamlet* by Shakespeare. For the
                  University of Canterbury Drama
                  Society at the Civic Theatre.

24 July 1959   *Antony and Cleopatra* by Shakespeare.
                  For the University of Canterbury
                  Drama Society at the Civic Theatre.

27 July 1962   *Macbeth* by Shakespeare. For the
                  University of Canterbury Drama
                  Society at the Civic Theatre.

19 July 1963   *King Henry IV Part One* by Shakespeare.
                  For the University of Canterbury
                  Drama School at the Civic Theatre.

17 July 1964   *Julius Caesar* by Shakespeare. For the
                  University of Canterbury Drama
                  Society at the Civic Theatre.

19 April 1965   *Two's Company*. For the Canterbury
                  Repertory Society at the Provincial
                  Council Chamber.

1967   *Twelfth Night* by Shakespeare. For the
                  University of Canterbury Drama
                  Society at the Ngaio Marsh Theatre
                  (Inaugural production).

14 June 1969   *A Midsummer Night's Dream* by
                  Shakespeare. For the University of
                  Canterbury Drama Society at the
                  Ngaio Marsh Theatre.

14 Nov 1970   *The Magistrate* by Arthur W. Pinero.
                  For the Canterbury Reperatory
                  Theatre Society.

01 Oct 1972   *King Henry V* by Shakespeare. For the
Christchurch Town Hall Committee
for the Combined Theatre Societies
of Canterbury at the James Hay
Theatre (Inaugural production).

1976   *Sweet Mr Shakespeare* devised by
Jonathan Elsom and written by
Ngaio Marsh. At the Court Theatre.

A Bibliography of Detective Novels by Ngaio Marsh

A Man Lay Dead. London: Geoffrey Bles, 1934; New York: Sheridan, 1942.

Enter A Murderer. London: 1935; New York: Pocket Books, 1941.

The Nursing-Home Murder (with Henry Jellett). London: Geoffrey Bles, 1935; New York: Sheridan, 1941.

Death in Ecstasy. London: Geoffrey Bles, 1936; New York: Sheridan, 1941.

Vintage Murder. London: Geoffrey Bles, 1937; New York: Sheridan, 1940.

Artists in Crime. London: Geoffrey Bles and New York: Furman, 1938.

Death in a White Tie. London: Geoffrey Bles and New York: Furman, 1938.

Overture to Death. London: William Collins and New York: Furman, 1939.

241

Death at the Bar. London: William Collins and Boston: Little Brown, 1940.

Death of a Peer. Boston: Little Brown, 1940; as *Surfeit of Lampreys*, London: William Collins, 1941.

Death and the Dancing Footman. Boston: Little Brown, 1941; London: William Collins, 1942.

Colour Scheme. London: William Collins and Boston: Little Brown, 1943.

Died in the Wool. London: William Collins and Boston: Little Brown, 1945.

Final Curtain. London: William Collins and Boston: Little Brown, 1947.

Swing, Brother, Swing. London: William Collins, 1949; as *A Wreath for Rivera*, Boston: Little Brown, 1949.

Opening Night. London: William Collins, 1951; as *Night at the Vulcan*, Boston: Little Brown, 1951.

Spinsters in Jeopardy. Boston: Little Brown, 1953; London: William Collins, 1954; as *The Bride of Death*, New York: Spivak, 1955.

Scales of Justice. London: William Collins and Boston: Little Brown, 1955.

Death of a Fool. Boston, Little Brown, 1956; as *Off with His Head*, London: William Collins, 1957.

Singing in the Shrouds. Boston: Little Brown, 1958; London: William Collins, 1959.

False Scent. Boston: Little Brown and London: William Collins, 1960.

Hand in Glove. Boston: Little Brown and London: William Collins, 1962.

Dead Water. Boston: Little Brown, 1963; London: William Collins, 1964.

Killer Dolphin. Boston: Little Brown, 1966; as *Death at the Dolphin,* London: William Collins, 1967.

Clutch of Constables. London: William Collins, 1968; Boston: Little Brown, 1969.

When in Rome. London: William Collins, 1970; Boston, Little Brown, 1971.

Tied Up in Tinsel. London: William Collins and Boston: Little Brown, 1972.

Black as He's Painted. London: William Collins and Boston: Little Brown, 1974.

Last Ditch. Boston: Little Brown and London: William Collins, 1977.

Grave Mistake. Boston: Little Brown and London: William Collins, 1978.

Photo Finish. London: William Collins and Boston: Little
    Brown, 1980.

Light Thickens. London: William Collins and Boston:
    Little Brown, 1982.

A Bibliography of Short Crime Stories
by Ngaio Marsh

"The Figure Quoted," *The Christchurch Sun*, Christmas, 1927; O. N. Gillespie, ed., *New Zealand Short Stories.* London: Dent, 1930.

"Death on the Air," *The Grand Magazine*, December 1934; Ellery Queen, ed., *Anthology 1969.* New York: Davis, 1968.

" I Can Find My Way Out," *Ellery Queen Mystery Magazine*, August 1946; Ellery Queen, ed., *Queen's Awards 1946.* Boston: Little Brown, and London: Gollancz, 1946.

"The Cupid Mirror," Susan Dickson, ed., *The Drugged Cornet and Other Mystery Stories.* New York: Dutton, 1972.

"Chapter and Verse," *Ellery Queen Mystery Magazine*, March 1973; *Ellery Queen's Murdercade.* New York: Random House, 1975.

"A Fool About Money," *Ellery Queen Mystery Magazine*, December 1974; *Ellery Queen's Crime Wave.* New York: Putnam, 1976.

"Morepork," Julian Symons, ed., *Verdict of Thirteen.* Harper & Row, 1978.

Notes on Contributors

Catherine Aird is the author of a well known series of detective novels featuring Inspector C. D. (Seedy) Sloan of the Calleshire CID. Very much a man in the middle, Sloan is leant on from above by Superintendent Leeyes and not very ably supported from below by "Defective" Constable Crosby. Aird claims that any resemblance between her fictional Calleshire and her native Kent is purely coincidental, although there is a newel post in her home like the murder weapon used in *The Religious Body*. A former chairman of the Crime Writers Association, she is one of the editors of the *Oxford Companion to Crime and Mystery Writing* and is also writing a biography of Josephine Tey.

Paul R. Bushnell is a director, playwright, performing arts critic, and broadcaster on opera and music-theatre for New Zealand's classical music station Concert FM. Granted a British Council award for the study of educational drama in the United Kingdom in 1988, he founded the Canterbury Association for Drama in Education, and has led preservice courses in drama for teaching trainees. He has been a research fellow at the University of Canterbury, researching and testing methods of assessing drama, and he presently teaches the subject at Linwood High School, Christchurch, where he also directs the Linwood Performing Arts Centre. He has written and performed a sequence of recitals tracing the New Zealand experience of Christmas, and his play for young people

Bright Fine Gold comes out in 1995. He is about to join Concert FM, Radio New Zealand, as producer of spoken features. He is a member of the Christchurch committee organizing the 1995 centenary of Dame Ngaio Marsh's birth.

John Dacres-Mannings is Ngaio Marsh's cousin and principal heir. A native New Zealander, he was educated at Christ's College Christchurch, an English-style public school. During his school days, a close bond with Dame Ngaio developed. He appears as a young man sharing the pleasures of London in her autobiography, *Black Beech and Honeydew*. In 1953, he was commissioned into the Royal Artillery and, briefly, the Scots Guards. He served with the British Army of the Rhine and was invalided out in 1961. He is currently a merchant banker in Australia.

Alzina Stone Dale is a freelance writer and lecturer who lives in the Victorian house in which she grew up in Chicago, Illinois. Among her many publications are the *Mystery Readers Walking Guide: Chicago* (1995)--as well as one for London, for England, and for New York. During 1994 she gave talks on scenes of the crime in mystery fiction at over 50 libraries in the Chicago area, acted as guide for her own Chicago Mystery Bus Tours, conducted workshops for Urban Gateways, and taught Lyceum seminars at the Newberry Library. She has written works on G. K. Chesterton (*The Outline of Sanity, A Life of G. K. Chesterton,* 1982) and T. S. Eliot (*T. S. Eliot, the Philosophy Poet,* 1988). In addition, she has published three books on Dorothy L. Sayers: a biography, *Maker and Craftsman* (1978, rev. ed. 1992); an edition of Sayers's comedies, *Love All* (1984); and a collection of essays, *Dorothy L. Sayers, The Centenary Celebration* (1993).

Douglas G. Greene is the author or editor of twelve books, ranging from studies of L. Frank Baum's Oz books to analyses of Seventeenth-Century British History. He is editor of four collections of John Dickson Carr's short stories, an anthology entitled *Death Locked In*, and *The Collected Short Fiction of Ngaio Marsh*. His biography, *John Dickson Carr: The Man Who Explained Miracles* was published by Otto Penzler Books (March 1995). He is currently Director of the Institute of Humanities at Old Dominion University.

Bruce Harding has the distinction of being the first person to write a Ph.D. thesis on Ngaio Marsh in New Zealand. He has published articles on Marsh in *Landfall* and *Australian and New Zealand Studies in Canada*. He is a Fellow of the Macmillan Brown Centre for Pacific Studies at the University of Canterbury in Christchurch, N. Z., and teaches in the English Department at the Christchurch Boys' High School. He is a member of the committee organizing the centenary celebrations of Ngaio Marsh's birth in Christchurch.

H. R. F. Keating has been writing crime fiction since 1959. He is the creator of the series featuring Inspector Ghote of the Bombay CID, and his awards include both a Golden Dagger from the Crime Writers Association and an Edgar conferred by the Mystery Writers of America. He is not only the current President of the Detection Club (whose history he is compiling), as well as past chairman of the Crime Writers Association and the Society of Authors, but is also a well known reviewer and critic.

Dr. Margaret Lewis was born in Northern Ireland and grew up on the Canadian prairies. After studying at the University of Alberta, she went to Leeds where she studied modern literature, in particular, new literatures written in English. Her doctoral thesis, taken at the University of Newcastle, was written on the Australian novelist Patrick White. She has taught for the Open University, the Workers' Educational Association, and for a number of universities on a part-time basis. *Ngaio Marsh: A Life* was published in London and New Zealand in 1991. Her latest book on the life and work of Ellis Peters was published in October 1994 by Seren Press.

Kathryne Slate McDorman received her Ph. D. in British History from Vanderbilt University. Since 1977 she has been a Professor of British History at Texas Christian University in Fort Worth, Texas. She has written several articles on how historians may use fiction to ascertain the underlying ideas and unconscious assumptions and prejudices of the people that buy it and read it. In 1991 she published the first biographical and critical study about Ngaio Marsh in the United States. Her current research interests are focused upon war correspondents in Britain in the late nineteenth century.

Susan Oleksiw is the author of the Mellingham Mystery series featuring Chief of Police Joe Silva, published by Scribner's (*Murder in Mellingham* (1993), *Double Take* (1994), and *Family Album* (1995). Her reviews and essays appear in *The Drood Review of Mystery* and *Mystery Scene*, as well as newspapers and magazines in the Boston area, where she also teaches courses on writing and literature at various colleges. Her first publication in the mystery field was *A Reader's Guide to the Classic British Mystery* (G. K. Hall, 1988), the first in a series of readers' guides for which she is editor. Susan received a Ph.D. in Sanskrit from the University of Pennsylvania, and has lived and traveled extensively in India.

B. A. Pike is a retired teacher and occasional lecturer on crime fiction. He is the author of *Campion's Career* (1987), a critical study of Margery Allingham, and *Detective Fiction: The Collector's Guide* (with John Cooper, 1988; 2nd ed. 1994). He is a contributor to *A Review of English Literature, Books and Bookmen, The Armchair Detective,* and *Twentieth Century Crime and Mystery Writing.* He is an advisor for the *Oxford Companion to Crime and Mystery Writing*

B. J. Rahn is an Associate Professor of English at Hunter College of the City University of New York. She has been teaching, researching, and writing about detective fiction for over a decade. She is co-founder and editor of *Murder Is Academic,* a newsletter for people teaching crime fiction at colleges and universities. She has published numerous articles on detective fiction and edited a collection of syllabi of courses on the genre. She serves as an advisor for the *Oxford Companion to Crime and Mystery Writing.* She is a member of the Mystery Writers of America, the Crime Writers Association of the U. K., the Sherlock Holmes Society of London, and the Dorothy L. Sayers Society.

Marilyn Rye is Assistant Professor of English and Director of Freshman Writing at Fairleigh Dickinson University, Madison, New Jersey. Her recent anthology, *Making Cultural Connections,* uses multi-cultural texts to develop critical thinking in composition courses. In addition to her scholarship in the field of composition, Dr. Rye has written on detective fiction, American women writers, and native American literature.

Julian Symons is probably equally admired as a crime novelist, reviewer, and critic. In addition to writing traditional detective fiction, he also perfected the villain-centered story--

like *The Man Who Killed Himself*--in which the central character is ironically foiled by his own chicanery. His critical studies include biographies of Edgar Allan Poe, Arthur Conan Doyle, and Dashiell Hammett and his history of the genre, *Bloody Murder: From the Detective Story to the Crime Novel*. A founder member of the Crime Writers Association, he served as its chairman and as president of the Detection Club and of the Conan Doyle Society. He was granted both the Golden Dagger and Diamond Dagger awards by the CWA.